*Northrop Frye in Modern Criticism*

# Northrop Frye

## in Modern Criticism

\*

*Selected Papers*
*from the English Institute*

EDITED WITH AN INTRODUCTORY
ESSAY BY MURRAY KRIEGER

COLUMBIA UNIVERSITY PRESS

NEW YORK *&* LONDON

1966

Acknowledgment is made to Alfred A. Knopf, Inc., for permission to quote four lines from "Lytton Strachey, Also, Enters into Heaven," by Wallace Stevens, published in *Opus Posthumous;* to Harcourt, Brace & World, Inc., for permission to quote from Northrop Frye's *Fables of Identity;* and to Random House, Inc., for permission to quote six lines from Karl Shapiro's *Essay on Rime,* copyright 1945 by Karl Shapiro.

# Foreword

W H E N  R. W. B. Lewis, then Chairman of the English Institute, asked me to organize this first formal assessment of Northrop Frye's work, I immediately felt both exhilarated and fearful about the prospect of my task. Exhilarated by the challenge of finding conclusive and yet varied judgments of a figure whose pervasive influence has made the rendering of such judgments— even at this early date—a necessary service; fearful because of the need to find treatments at once admiring, critical, and just— especially with the subject of these papers still so actively among us, as recent Institute conferences and volumes have attested. Indeed, from the first it was hoped that he could be induced—as he has been—to respond to the three central papers. So although Mr. Frye, for reasons made clear in his "Letter" which introduced our proceedings, chose to be absent from our deliberations, he is present upon the occasion of this volume, which is the record and the projection of that earlier occasion.

In assigning the three papers I meant to achieve a rather ob-vious balance: a paper by a writer influenced by Mr. Frye who would want to defend the master's work and its consequences, a paper dedicated to respectful dissent, and a paper—less committed to a position—that might transcend the polemic or perhaps remove it by offering an alternative perspective. This is the order of the papers delivered by Angus Fletcher, W. K. Wimsatt, and Geoffrey H. Hartman. Messrs. Wimsatt's and Hartman's papers appear here substantially in the form in which they were originally delivered, while Mr. Fletcher has undertaken some revisions.

But other materials are included here as well. I have already mentioned Mr. Frye's "Letter" which opened our proceedings and the response he kindly consented to write which now concludes them. The nature of our undertaking convinced me also that a checklist of works by and about Mr. Frye would increase its usefulness enormously. But, in asking my colleague, John E. Grant, to provide this checklist, I could hardly have anticipated the awe-inspiring energy which he would bring to his chore or the amazing fullness of his findings, so that only now do I conceive how indispensable a contribution the checklist is. Finally there is my own introductory essay. It was written, like Mr. Frye's response, in awareness of the three papers delivered at the conference, although—because of the press of time—neither Mr. Frye nor I was able to see the other's essay before writing his own.

I thought it would be wrong for me, in introducing these papers, to steal the thunder or rainbows from them by giving too rich a foretaste of their words and ideas in my own. Still, being familiar with them and convinced of their high quality, I may well have borrowed from their searching awareness, even if unconsciously. My primary intention, however, has been to relate

Northrop Frye to our responses rather than to theirs. For the papers by Messrs. Fletcher, Wimsatt, and Hartman concentrated upon Mr. Frye's work with such intensity that they could manage but slight opportunity to relate that work to contemporary criticism and to the critical tradition at large. Yet his relation to contemporary criticism constituted half our title and subject. In order to give this aspect of our subject the central attention its importance calls for, I have taken the liberty of writing an extended essay.

The task assigned me is now completed, but I still feel the exhilaration and the fear with which I began. That the task was at all feasible can be attributed to the talents and devotion of the three major contributors and our bibliographer, and to the warm cooperation of Northrop Frye, who allowed himself to become at once our subject and our collaborator, of former Chairman R. W. B. Lewis, of Scott Elledge, his successor, and of the Supervising Committee of the Institute. I join readers of this volume in extending thanks to them.

Murray Krieger

*University of Iowa*
*February, 1966*

# *Contents*

Foreword     v

MURRAY KRIEGER

Northrop Frye and Contemporary Criticism: Ariel and the
Spirit of Gravity     1

MURRAY KRIEGER / *University of Iowa*

Letter to the English Institute, 1965     27

NORTHROP FRYE / *University of Toronto*

Utopian History and the *Anatomy of Criticism*     31

ANGUS FLETCHER / *Columbia University*

Northrop Frye: Criticism as Myth     75

W. K. WIMSATT / *Yale University*

Ghostlier Demarcations     109

GEOFFREY H. HARTMAN / *Cornell University*

Reflections in a Mirror                                        133
    NORTHROP FRYE

A Checklist of Writings by and about Northrop Frye            147
    JOHN E. GRANT / *University of Iowa*

Supervising Committee, 1965                                   189

Program                                                       191

Registrants                                                   195

*Northrop Frye in Modern Criticism*

# Murray Krieger

\*

## Northrop Frye & Contemporary Criticism

### ARIEL AND THE SPIRIT

### OF GRAVITY

T H E three essays which follow were originally conceived and written independently of one another, and within only a most general format. They could be expected only coincidentally to make up a total consideration of their subject. Consequently, it seemed to me that I might best introduce and organize them by creating a context for them: by commenting both on the theoretical situation upon which that extraordinary volume, the *Anatomy of Criticism,* made its extraordinary impact and on the aftermath of that impact.

Whatever the attitude toward Northrop Frye's prodigious scheme, one cannot doubt that, in what approaches a decade since the publication of his masterwork, he has had an influence —indeed an absolute hold—on a generation of developing literary critics greater and more exclusive than that of any one theorist in recent critical history. One thinks of other movements that have held sway, but these seem not to have depended so completely on a single critic—nay, on a single work—as has the criticism in the work of Frye and his *Anatomy*. For example, pervasive as was T. S. Eliot's influence, it joined almost at once and indistinguishably with that of a number of followers who tried to systematize the master's casual essays drawn together from here and there. But with Frye, there is no difficulty disengaging master from disciple, nor even Frye's own later and lesser works from the masterwork. His followers and his ensuing works produce in the main simplifications and extensions of—even footnotes to—the *Anatomy,* the Word propagated and translated, thinned in order to be spread.

The unequaled sweep with which the *Anatomy* has gathered to itself our theoretical imaginations is largely due to the unequaled sweep with which it claims to embrace our entire conceptual world. Frye's incomparable power among many of us may well be traced, as Geoffrey Hartman suggests, to his universalism, his system-making daring, his unmitigated theoretical ambition, his unlimited reach—even where some would say it has exceeded his grasp. His power may be traced also, as Angus Fletcher and Hartman both suggest, to his revitalizing the flow of a romantic sensibility and vision that the critical tradition after Eliot, with the austerity of its would-be classicism, had too long congealed. Fletcher well reminds us that Frye terms himself an *Odyssey* rather than an *Iliad* critic; and Hartman credits him with the recovery of romance for us all as well as with the recovery of the romantic arrogance that strives for the universal completeness of a man-centered, man-created logos. There is a satisfying lack of inhibition in the cosmic pretension with which Frye permits the imagination to chart the galaxies dreamed of by human desires. And this pretension, in its very recklessness, has seized the imagination of the rest of us, long inhibited by the unyielding finitude flung upon us like a blanket by the critical tradition of T. E. Hulme and Eliot. The audacity of Frye's mythophilia is an alternative appealing through the very assertion of its autonomy. Responsible only to itself and, thus, to our dreams of wish-fulfillment, the free-ranging mythic universe shifts its galaxies at will to answer every need. It freely rotates in patterns beyond the fixed sublunary purposes of our pedestrian interests which require the universe to stand still. As pedestrians, we persist in hunting for equations, echoes, parallels, or just analogues among Frye's schematic groupings; and we do find some—or *almost* do, but not quite. Shifts in axis give each of his constellations a different center. Together they elude our two-dimensional spatial need to systematize and thus assimilate them.

Such diagrammatic attempts to freeze the dynamic fluidity of Frye's categories account for the simplifications and reductions that Frye's followers and opponents have worked on the original grand mythic scheme in order to make it hold still either to be applied or to be attacked. And his followers have been at least as guilty as his opponents. Indeed on occasion his own more popularly directed essays have as seriously sacrificed the earlier shifting fullness of his entire scheme. It is true, of course, that critics who tried to take Frye whole could not then put him to their uses; they could only apprehend him aesthetically as having the unusable completeness of a poetic entity. So it must for the most part be said that we have not been responding to the totality of his modes in their own deceptive movements so much as we have been, as followers, adapting his work or, as antagonists, disposing of it for our own more parochial purposes. However we have been using him by putting him to *our* tests, we have not paused sufficiently to accommodate ourselves to him or him to the total march of critical theory. Few except the most faithful (and these therefore too uncritically) have selflessly tried to uncover the source of his power, together with the cost—the expense in theoretical soundness—which that power exacts. We must attempt that critical search, however, with a daring that matches his daring if not, alas, with a wit that matches his wit.

The educational concerns of Frye and the educational possibilities of his work have been largely responsible for the reduction of certain isolated aspects of his theories into fixed and simplified programs. His large-scale categorizing, the tendency to outline, the invention of a nomenclature—all have misled the pseudo-scientific among his followers into making of him a framework for teaching and for literary study. Programmatic applications have begun to appear in places like *College English* and in textbooks, and we can expect more of them. Frye's admitted propensity to spatialize literature has led others to spatialize him, to flatten him into the firmness of diagram. But often there is too little awareness that his space can be Einsteinian, its relations defiant of the two-dimensional page, its categories as slippery as time itself. Frye is far more difficult and deceptive than others have often made him or than he has often made himself in writings after the *Anatomy*. Too frequently, then, the swirling galaxies of Frye's autonomous universe have been fixed in a single position, as by geocentric man, in accordance with the *terra firma* commanded by pedagogic interests. And what made that universe so uniquely provocative—its elusive, free-swinging character—is lost.

The sublunary concerns of rival theorists have led them to be similarly partial. Without his dedication to an autonomous projection of a universal schematics,[1] his antagonists have had to reduce him to the traditional terms that have guided the history of more modest critical theory.[2] The essay by W. K. Wimsatt amply and effectively demonstrates the several varieties I shall enumerate of the traditional theorists' impatience with Frye. With their traditional theoretical criteria, they have manifested their distrust of what they see as his too great trust in an eccentric and arbitrary pseudo-logos. There has been the general complaint that Frye's shifting categories produce, not the brilliant dynamics of dialectic, but the sloppiness of inconsistency; but the complaint is accompanied by admiring bafflement at his sleight-of-hand, at the way

[1] Originally I thought of using *systematics* instead of *schematics* here. But, as Frye points out in his respondent essay to this volume (which I took the editor's privilege of reading before my remarks went to press), his categories and modes might better be thought of as schematic than as systematic creations. The word *system,* used effectively by Hartman at the start of his essay, suggests too regular and philosophically consistent a structure for the bold, imaginative, often system-defying structures of a poet-theorist like Frye.

[2] My own earlier treatment of Frye (*A Window to Criticism: Shakespeare's Sonnets and Modern Poetics* [Princeton, 1964], pp. 42–49, 207*n*) is representative of this partial view of Frye's multiple schemes, a view that limits him to what one's own limited position would make of him. I am not confessing to being wrong so much as to treating him only in so far as this treatment was relevant to the fixed concerns of the modern critical tradition. Since his is a revolution against this tradition, both in substance and in attitude, against its conception of the very nature of critical discourse, my terms could not be meant to be relevant to *his* totality.

he evades the reductive and spatial impulse that wants to "place" him. More specifically, there has, first, been the complaint that he neglects, and at times flatly denies, the critic's task of evaluation; but the complaint is often accompanied by the acknowledgment that he sometimes speaks effectively about taste and judgment. There has, secondly, been the complaint that, in centering upon the *literary* relations of literature, he irrevocably separates literature from its relation to life, from its mimetic responsibility; but the complaint is often accompanied by the admission that he, sometimes uneasily, wants it tied to life, even in the name of mimesis. It has thus been charged that, while he emphasizes now one and now the other of these desirable opposites, he cannot fuse them systematically; that he has not shown how, "the actual being only a part of the possible," "literature . . . neither *reflects* nor *escapes* from ordinary life." [3] There has, thirdly, been the complaint that Frye's archetypal interests cheat the individual work of its uniqueness by seeing it only as another translation of the universal story; but this complaint should be accompanied by an awareness that Frye does attend to detailed meaning-functions in the more minute levels or "phases" which he attributes to the many-leveled literary symbol. Or, to move in the other direction, we should remember that the archetypal gives way to the all-involving anagogic phase which carries in itself the potential identity of every part of man's myth, both before and in the in-dividual work: the microcosm become macrocosm, but—as always in the circular pattern—only as the converse is also true. The movement from literal to archetype and from archetype to an-agoge, as it swirls, deprives us of these complaints. Still it allows

[3] *The Well-Tempered Critic* (Bloomington, 1963), p. 155, my italics.

us, in our sublunary language, to complain now about what we insist on terming inconsistency, discursive irresponsibility, even if our Blakean poet-critic claims, in his lunar dialectic, to soar beyond our downward pull. For example, we find Wimsatt condemning Frye on the one hand for being too Chicagoan in his multiplication of differentiated categories, on the other hand for being too Platonic in his archetypal universals that blur all distinctions and all particulars, and, beyond both, for allowing the two jarring inadequacies to become inconsistencies as well. But what we learn we are learning about Wimsatt and the habits of the traditional theoretical intelligence as well as about the will-o'-the-wisp imagination of the poet-as-theorist or theorist-as-poet.

To reckon honestly and totally with Frye, then, to uncover the source and the cost of his power, we must for the occasion soar with him to his lunar universe with its modes that change their faces and shift their places in accordance with a reckless dialectic of dream that shades every point we focus upon and slides across our sober, sublunary, daytime complaints. It is precisely the opposition of the lunar to the sublunary that characterizes Frye's flight from the dominant critical tradition—from Hulme through Eliot to the New Critics—that preceded the fervent revolution he perpetrated. His departure accounts for the true basis of their resistance to him and his sway. About no claim are those I once termed "the new apologists for poetry" more constant or even dogged than the claim that poetry should reveal, and should be limited by, our worldly experience: what Dr. Johnson called "the real state of sublunary nature," product of what Keats called "the dull brain [that] perplexes and retards." These theorists speak as with one voice for the true poet's capacity to respect the drag of material reality, to convert the handicaps of a finite existence and a finite language into victories of an imagination that never forgets or rejects its basis in common experience.

Their early spokesman, Hulme, may have been their most intemperate in his attack on romanticism by way of his defense of classicism:

> What I mean by classical in verse, then, is this. That even in the most imaginative flights there is always a holding back, a reservation. The classical poet never forgets this finiteness, this limit of man. He remembers always that he is mixed up with earth. He may jump, but he always returns back; he never flies away into the circumambient gas.
>
> You might say if you wished that the whole of the romantic attitude seems to crystallise in verse round metaphors of flight. Hugo is alway flying, flying over abysses, flying up into the eternal gases. The word infinite in every other line.

We can see his nearly violent scorn translate what I have been calling Frye's lunar universe of swirling galaxies into "circumambient gas." But in Hulme's extreme statement we can see the basis for the theoretical antagonism to Frye's romantic creativity —a classicist might call it romantic escapism—by the critical tradition he has pretty well supplanted. The antagonism can be traced to the unromantic doctrine of the Fall of man which leads the Hulmean to call for earthbound man to recognize and even celebrate his limitations and to avoid the humanist's arrogance that, denying the Fall, disdains the earth for the arbitrary heavens of his own creation.

One after another of the New Apologists pays tribute to the poet's capacity to dedicate himself to his material finitude. We can recall that John Crowe Ransom related the unique power of poetry to the rich contingency of the world's body in its earthy density. Poetry for Ransom shows its power by devoting itself to—not evading—the furniture of our world, its dull, burdensome obstacles to our will to flight. We can project what would be his opposition to Frye from his early attack on "Platonic poetry," where he joins the battle for *Dinglichkeit* against a disembodied utopia. Or Allen Tate makes his doctrine of "tension" begin at its lower end with literal reality, no matter how transcendent the symbolic levels into which it opens. In his later work "tension" becomes the "symbolic imagination," which, beginning from the "common thing," "carries the bottom along with it, however high it may climb." The inadequate alternative to the symbolic imagination is the "angelic imagination," which bypasses the earthly, overleaps and cheats the condition of man, "in the illusory pursuit of essence." This "angelism of the intellect," performed by a Frye-like creature too anxious to renounce his sensuous being and to become angel instead of man, can be seen as the poetic weakness deriving from Gnosticism. Or we can recall Eliseo Vivas' constant insistence on the poet's chief obligation to the "primary data of experience." Or my own claim that the ultimate function of a contextual poetry is to provide existential revelation.

The dedication to the existential is often accompanied, in the modern critical tradition, by the interest in the tragic and the ironic. The difference in Frye's emphasis can be seen point by point. He condemns "existential projection" as the false attempt to destroy the autonomy of the literary universe by reducing it to our lowly experiential world. For literature to pursue a relation between itself and the existential would be, for Frye, an abdication of its high destiny, of its obligation to minister to the creative human desire rather than to open for us the destructive realities of the human condition. Literature is made out of prior literature, not life; it yields poetic, mythic categories, not existential ones. The relation of a central tragic concern to our existential sense seems clear enough from what has been said; this concern can be followed as a major theme in recent criticism before Frye. That his own work centers on comedy and romance, spring and summer, rather than the autumn of tragedy, Fletcher and Hartman, as I have said, make abundantly clear in their essays. Frye dwells on rebirth and not death, not on the descent to the underworld but on the return and the upward movement within the circle which man uses to construct his sense of his destiny. Similarly, irony, which became so conclusive a literary (and existential) quality for critics before Frye, is by him seen as the lowest reach of the downward movement of displacement from pure myth, to be gone through almost before we arrive at it; for irony derives its major excitement for Frye from our capacity to see in it, paradoxically, the beginnings of the upward movement that can return us to the undisguised gods.

Frye and the modern critical tradition, then, should, in their opposition, come to be recognized as utter alternatives, indeed as very little less than mutually exclusive. In spite of my earlier worries about the inadequacy of diagrams in dealing with Frye, let me try the accompanying diagram as an immediate indication of this opposition between him and the modern critical tradition.

In traditional modern theory the critic is seen as viewing the individual work in its relations to the actual world of experience (including the world of art) even as that world is in part defined by the work in its internal relations. The endless variations among

such theories depend on how these relations achieve their defini-
tions and their priorities. According to the revolutionary theory
of Frye the critic is first seen making a downward movement to
the work and the world. This movement is an echo of the downward movement toward displacement and the reality principle

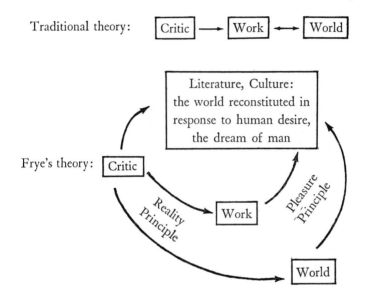

that literature makes in its historical movement from unencum-
bered myth through mimetic forms to irony, although with the
latter's promise to return. For myth, like a god, enters history's
downward path, marching through history in a variety of displaced forms before the eschatological return to oneness. The
critic too moves through the lowering displacements of the individual work, the limitations placed on its meanings and movements by its discreteness, its persistent attempt to become a
unique self-enclosure. As man, the critic makes a similar down-

ward movement through the unresponsive realities of the unelevated sublunary world. But there is an answering upward
movement and return, as in the archetypes of rebirth and of the
quest myth: the critic moves from the individuated work, as man
moves from the unenlightened world, upward to his imaginative
home, which is their (the work's and the world's) imaginative
transposition. This is the world as remade by human desire,
man's dream, which as creative act makes a world in which man
chooses to live. If the critic's downward movement is made in
accordance with the reality principle, the upward movement is
made in accordance with the pleasure principle—pleasure rendered innocent as the creation of unfallen man. Thus Freud's
development and hierarchy, from pleasure to reality, are reversed.
The critic moves from displacements, in their variations seen in
multiple singleness, to the pure revelations of the oneness into
which all single variations empty. It is as if the work and the
sublunary world, suffering similarly under the curse of the Fall,
the curse of individuation, were—with critic as midwife—reborn
as the Platonic One of which all human experience and all art
are in quest.

But the other arrow from the critic indicates that he has also
moved to this world-as-dream directly, in an upward movement
of unmediated vision. I have warned earlier of the spatial inadequacies of diagrams applied to Frye's schematics. In my diagram of the critic's movements we also find space betrayed and
deepened by time. For the critic has had his world of culture—
created by himself as poet—prepared all the time for the ascent
from the individual work and the world. Until this point we
have described the critic as making two movements. First, down-

ward: he has, as critic, descended to the work and, as man, he has descended to the world (indeed, he has descended to what, from the view on high, seems to be the underworld). But, preparing to make his second movement, the upward return, he need not relate work and world to one another, since both are to be dissolved into something higher. At this stage the literary work is seen only as it is related to the world of literature, of culture, of dream; only as it evolves out of literary causes. For the fallen world must be raised rather than allowed the praise of art; it must be transformed and not transcribed. Neither subject nor object, the fallen world is what poetry—in its creation of its properly human subject and object—must leap across. But now we discover that there has also been a third movement all along, made prior to and independently of the others, even as it is also made simultaneously with them. The downward and upward movements arrive at the place where the critic has always been, a place to which he must always immediately move. Out of the work and the world, out of the downward movements made by both critic as critic and critic as man, both critic and man make the return to the imaginative world, to the world as man wills to have it, although it is the very world which, as Blakean poet, he has already created from the beginning.

In contrast, then, to the careful distinctions among entities, functions, subject and object drawn by traditional modern theory, in Frye subject, object, and universal—critic, man, poet, work, world, and literature or world-as-dream—all merge into the One that receives all, the One that the world-as-dream becomes even as it becomes the all-transforming creative act of man. No wonder critics in the wake of Frye have devoted themselves increasingly

to "vision" and visionaries, to romantic and utopist poet-philoso-
phers. Further, since his notion of epiphany does permit Frye to
leave open the possibility of a momentary break-through of the
desired into the real, of utopia into the resistant world of things,
his position can—like an earlier romanticism—have immediate
political consequences for those who are in earnest about the
egalitarian possibilities of the "classless" society. In all these
respects, a vision is being pressed that apparently seeks to define,
in the extremest terms possible, the humanist and romantic attitude which Hulme so bitterly denounced in the name of the
classic and Christian traditions. It is as if Hulme's too simple
caricature of romanticism had truly created itself out of his projections and now reached back to haunt the tradition he so
sternly sought to protect. As Hulme saw it would have to be,
the romantic attitude is born with the denial that the Fall can
touch the human imagination; and this denial leads to the arro-
gant assertion that man creates, *ex nihilo,* like a god, out of his
desires. —And he saw everything that he had made, and, behold,
it was very good.— For in that creation man has eluded the
traps of the fallen world of experience which would desecrate
the innocence of imagination. This imagination is enabled to
dream its golden dreams in its transcendence of the brazen world
that, in its spirit of gravity, exerts a downward pull.

If the words "golden" and "brazen" recall us to Sidney's *Apology for Poetry,* it is as it should be, since Frye's use of Sidney's
opposition of the golden world to the brazen world has been with
us from the beginning. Frye's multiple schemes have sought to
enclose nothing less than the entire history of human culture as
the history of the forms created by man's imagination; and the

forms, as archetypal, are seen to be controlled by the principle of eternal return. Therefore what could be more fitting than to approach the center, the *primum mobile,* of these multiple schemes than by way of Frye's own archetypal image? I find this image most clearly in the *Apology* of Sidney even as it came to him from Plato and passed from him to Shelley, though with less precision of adaptation than we find in Frye.

We can begin with Sidney's noted definition of the poet as being in no way limited to created nature but creating his own: ". . . onely the Poet . . . lifted up with the vigor of his owne invention, dooth growe in effect, another nature . . . so as hee goeth hand in hand with Nature, not inclosed within the narrow warrant of her guifts, but freely ranging onely within the Zodiack of his owne wit." The word "Zodiack" should bring us at once to the area of imagery I have been pressing in Frye,[4] that which Wimsatt reminds us of when he quotes Frye's vision of man's imagination building its "cities out of the Milky Way." But a bit later we find Sidney, in freeing the poet from subservience to fact (he need "borrow nothing of what is, hath been, or shall be"), frees him to "range onely rayned with learned discretion, into the divine consideration of what may be, and should be."

---

[4] In view of my own insistence on Frye's swirling galaxies and my attempt here to relate them to Sidney's "Zodiack of his owne wit," I must record the coincidental title of an essay by John Holloway, "The Critical Zodiac of Northrop Frye," *The Colours of Clarity* (London, 1964), pp. 153–60. This essay does not refer to Sidney or to the theoretical context of the *Apology,* and I came upon it after my own essay—largely grounded in the Sidney reference—was well under way; but I did find the Holloway title comforting. I am indebted to my colleague and this volume's bibliographer, John E. Grant, for pointing out this review of the *Anatomy.*

To range freely within the zodiac of one's own wit is apparently the same as ranging into the divine consideration of what may be and should be. Clearly wit, as imagination or invention, must be connected to the transcendent world of the ought-to-be. And so it is, in a quotation which comes between the two I have cited and allows one to be transposed to the other. Anxious lest his reader, in a Hulme-like mood, accuse him of elevating man and his wit to God's level, Sidney tries to account for creative man in a fallen universe:

Neyther let it be deemed too sawcie a comparison to ballance the highest poynt of mans wit with the efficacie of Nature: but rather give right honor to the heavenly Maker of that maker: who having made man to his owne likenes, set him beyond and over all the workes of that second nature, which in nothing hee sheweth so much as in Poetrie: when with the force of a divine breath, he bringeth things forth far surpassing her dooings, with no small argument to the incredulous of that first accursed fall of *Adam:* sith our erected wit, maketh us know what perfection is, and yet our infected will, keepeth us from reaching unto it.

In this properly Platonic concession, our wit is exempt from the Fall, although our will is thoroughly subject to it: our *"erected wit"* which can apprehend perfection and our *"infected will"* which cannot attain it. The brazen world of things as they are, the coarsening individuation of God's world, is the product of our infected will even though, within its zodiac, our erected wit can range freely, imagining the archetypal perfections of the golden world, the world before the Fall, Platonically governed by the divine considerations of things as they should be. For the erected wit, the free range within its zodiac can never be arbitrary but must automatically bring it to range within its archetypal home where the perfection of things as they should be works heavenly alchemy on the baser metals wrought by our sublunary will. For in its erect, upward-reaching state, the wit's zodiac is that of the Platonic heavens. The freedom from the Fall granted to wit is like that granted by Frye to his imagination. And it is like that which is found in Hulme's hostile definition of romanticism.

Sidney's elevated world of wit is the world of the poem, as high-flying and as anti-existential as Frye's. The world of things as they should be draws the zodiac of the poet's wit to merge with its own: it thus becomes the free creation of that wit. This world produces "in *Tantalus, Atreus,* and such like, nothing that is not to be shunned. In *Cyrus, Aeneas, Ulisses,* each thing to be followed. . . ." We seem to be in Frye's world of attraction and repulsion in accordance with desire, the wish-fulfillment that produces *his* things as they should be: the "demonic imagery" as "the presentation of the world that desire totally rejects" and its supernal opposite, the "apocalyptic imagery," "the categories of reality in the forms of human desire." [5] Further, as Sidney

[5] *Anatomy of Criticism* (Princeton, 1957), pp. 147 and 141. The golden world, for Frye as for Sidney, must always be defined by negative as well as positive fiats, by what we will not have as well as what we must have. Thus, in *The Educated Imagination* (Bloomington, 1964), pp. 98–100, as Frye extends literature beyond "only a wish-fulfillment dream" by turning to tragedy as well as to "romances and comedies with happy endings," it is only to show how literature deals with the negation of desire as well as desire, what we reject as well as what we want, nightmare as well as bliss. He can justify the horror of the blinding of Gloucester in *Lear* as "not the paralyzing sickening horror of a real blinding scene, but an exuberant horror, full of the energy of repudiation . . . as powerful a rendering as we

insists that the poet's should-be world is merely a "figuring forth," that "for the Poet, he nothing affirmes, and therefore never lyeth," that the stage "Thebes" is not the geographical "Thebes" because the poet speaks "not affirmatively, but allegorically, and figurativelie," we sense his closeness to Frye's insistence on the supposed, *as-if* world of literature: "Literature is a body of hypothetical thought and action: it makes, as literature, no statements or assertions." [6]

It should please Frye for us to have uncovered *his* archetype in some passages of Sidney.[7] Indeed, he should welcome our finding this early source as evidence of his claim that in the history of the human imagination all is new only as it is old, the new word but a new version of the old word, in the spirit of his own essay, "New Directions from Old." [8] He should of course be quick to

_____

can ever get of life as we don't want it." The "most vicious things" presented in literature produce an "exhilaration" from the fact that "they aren't really happening." Here we are—even in tragedy—in full flight from the world of experience to the world as we would have it or as we refuse to have it. The world of the literary imagination, Frye says in *The Well-Tempered Critic,* "is the universe in human form, stretching from the complete fulfillment of human desire to what human desire utterly repudiates" (p. 155).

[6] *The Well-Tempered Critic,* p. 149.

[7] Of course I am not claiming that Sidney is a unique source or that these doctrines are original with him. Further, one finds similar images in many places, if not within so similar and extensive a theoretical framework. One should notice, for example, that the development in America, in the nineteenth century, of the theory of fictional romance—as in many passages in the writings of Hawthorne and Henry James—is filled with heavenly and, more specifically, lunar imagery.

[8] In *Fables of Identity: Studies in Poetic Mythology* (New York, 1963), pp. 52–66.

point out two serious differences between Sidney and himself. First, Frye can go all the way to the golden world of man's wit and remain in it, while Sidney cannot systematically sustain his gesture to imagination since he is pulled back to the dully imitative by the conservative Italian critical tradition that claimed him. Frye has no Scaliger tugging at him to keep him from the total embrace of his grandest claims. Secondly and more basically, Frye explicitly and continually divorces his humanist-romantic attitude from all metaphysical claims, so that his golden world is the product only of the human imagination and has no other sanction.[9] Like Sidney's Platonic realm, Frye's zodiac of man's wit is related to the world as it should be. But this world has nothing of the metaphysically divine in it as it does for Sidney; the wit creates its zodiac which, responsive only to its creator, has no true home in the sky. So if one believes he can term Frye a Platonist, he must confront this crucial qualification to his claim, a qualification that might suggest Freud as an alternative influence. Freud rather than Jung, since Jung's archetypes also demand a metaphysic that Frye must reject. Frye's mythic gods, like Freud's neuroses, are related to our wishes and the frustration of these wishes, and in each case their displacement can give rise to literary creation. However, while displaced meaning is private for the Freudian poet, in response to secret wishes and secret frustrations, for Frye displaced meaning—like the wishes

[9] Frye himself distinguishes the romantic humanist from the Renaissance Christian humanist in terms of the latter's invocation of the Fall. See the important essay, "The Imaginative and the Imaginary," *Fables of Identity,* pp. 151–67, especially pp. 159–60. He seems, however, less aware of the metaphorical similarities between himself and Renaissance Platonism than he is of the metaphysical difference between them.

that create it—is universal and shared, the public property of the common human imagination which created and always re-creates those gods.[10] In this departure from Freud, Frye joins Sidney in celebrating the universals of the should-be world, despite his rejection of the metaphysical sanction for them as they are derived from Plato.

The relation of Frye to Plato, however incomplete, should recall us to Ransom's charge of Platonism and Tate's charge of "angelism" or Gnosticism against those who bypass the world of sense for an unmediated admission to the world of essence. Wimsatt's essay speaks similarly and with disfavor of Frye's "Gnostic mythopoeia." It is worth remembering that, in his conclusion to the *Literary Criticism: A Short History* (1957), on which he collaborated with Cleanth Brooks, Wimsatt spoke against both "the Platonic or Gnostic ideal world views" and "the Manichaean full dualism and strife of principles." The thirst for essence made the first too airy a flight from gravity, while the overabsorption in the evil of the fallen world kept the second too unelevated, too trapped in gravity's downward pull. As orthodox Christian, Wimsatt would resolve the two critical

[10] Frye can try to make his "desire" something more than either whim or the Freudian wish. Speaking of the imaginative in "The Imaginative and the Imaginary," in *Fables of Identity*, he can say, "The drive behind [the imaginative] we may call desire, a desire which has nothing to do with the biological needs and wants of psychological theory, but is rather the impulse toward what Aristotle calls *telos*, realizing the form that one potentially has" (p. 152). But this introduces a metaphysical dimension that he dare not develop, so that for him "desire" usually seems to carry its normal meanings and implications. He can urge but he cannot earn a distinction between "the creative and the neurotic."

heresies by way of the divine-earthly mystery of the Incarnation. His polemical writings that have followed this statement have pursued this double assault. Wimsatt has attacked existential critics like me for Manichaean tendencies, and now his linking of the anti-existential Frye to Gnosticism reveals him turning against the opposed critical (and theological) heresy. Further, Frye's humanistic liberation from Plato's metaphysic, the self-authentication of Frye's Gnostic tendencies, only compounds his error in Wimsatt's eyes.

We have seen that, in contrast to the dark archetypes of Jung, the archetypes of Frye have no metaphysical sanction. They are a humanistic construct of common man in search of his dream and creating it out of his need for wish-fulfillment. Thus the democratic universality of mythic structures is dependent on the universality, the commonness, of the structure of human desires —even to the ultimately universal dream of man, the "classless" civilization. But this would seem to be an empirical claim, subject to empirical evidence, and in need of an agreed-upon upward reading of the stories of our literature in the direction of spring and summer, as the quest for rebirth. In citing these two dominant archetypes of Frye, quest and rebirth, I suggest that unromantic readers are more convinced by death than rebirth, more convinced by the poverty they find than the pot of gold to which the rainbow promises to lead them in quest. Since obviously the history of our criticism has allowed many alternative readings of literature, we must realize that, far from meaning an empirical claim, Frye is rather creating, within the zodiac of *his* wit, galaxies that respond to his own poetic vision, even as his vision responds to Blake's. It is a vision, gorgeously complete in its dizzying schematics, that can be responded to by all celebrants of man in his spring and summer mood, the romantic singers of the golden world, the utopist questors for an Eden that nostalgia will not permit them quite to forget or forego and that irony will not permit them quite to attain for the fallen daytime world.

Frye's vision must then be seen as his own construct of the world of our literature in terms of his desires, as he would like it to be. What he gives us is the authorization, indeed the licensing, of what earlier positivistic theorists and philosophers disparagingly used to call the "emotive," as they worried about the primary role of wish-fulfillment in the structures of poets and of too-ambitious philosophers. In the fashion of the early I. A. Richards, they used "emotive" to outlaw poetry from the realm of meaningful discourse, and apologists for poetry protested by trying to demonstrate how poetry did give meaning to life. But Frye rather insists on the emotive as poetry's only content and would not have it otherwise; he celebrates poetry precisely for the characteristic that its old enemies proclaimed as its weakness and that its old friends sought to deny. And his licensing poetry according to this definition is also the licensing of his own way of theorizing—so revolutionary in its relation to the theoretical tradition—and of his theory itself as a massive poetic vision with all its swirling galaxies.

The lunar sweep of vision—beyond "Dull sublunary lovers' love,/ Whose soul is sense"—must prevent Frye from claiming, with many modern critics, that literature in the narrow sense has a unique role in creating that vision. For him the power of vision must be one with the power of the human imagination to create its structures, poetic or otherwise. The romantic imagination, in search of unmediated vision, must transcend the finite body of the poet's controlled precision in language just as we have seen it transcend the world's body itself. So my earlier diagram was designed to show. The philosopher, the critic—social-political as well as literary—must be admitted with the poet, so that, like Arnold before him, Frye is led outward from literature to culture and civilization at large, all of them products of imagination, nature (science's nature) given human form.

But it seems clear that Arnold was on solid ground when he made "culture," a total imaginative vision of life with literature at its center, the regulating and normalizing element in social life, the human source, at least, of spiritual authority. Culture in Arnold's sense is the exact opposite of an elite's game preserve; it is, in its totality, a vision or model of what humanity is capable of achieving, the matrix of all Utopias and social ideals.[11]

If Frye must liberate literature from sublunary experience, if, further, he must liberate the poet's imagination from bondage to the sublunary language allowed it by a Hulme-like critic, so he must liberate the critic from the stringent procedures of a sublunary critical discourse. For the critic also is an imaginative creator of a lunar world. As Frye—in deference to the ubiquity and primacy of vision—permits the literary imagination to expand to a culture's or a civilization's imagination, as he allows literature to expand to include all structures of thought, so he clearly must include the critical imagination within the literary, within what Blake termed the "poetic genius." The fidelity of the critical imagination must be first to its own free creatures, even before its fidelity to the creatures of others, of the poets, and surely

[11] *The Well-Tempered Critic,* p. 154.

before its fidelity to the bounds of critical discourse as agreed upon by the theoretical tradition from Aristotle to—shall we say—Wimsatt. To the last, Frye seems to demand systematic irresponsibility, a willful recklessness. For his is not only a revolutionary conception of the poet and of criticism, but a revolutionary conception of the nature and function of critical discourse. Whatever may be the accuracy of Wimsatt's assault on Frye's discursive methods, we must ask whether it is appropriate to Frye's elusive disdain for the methodological presuppositions which underlie all such assaults; whether it "is like trying a man by the laws of one country, who acted under those of another," as Pope said of neoclassical attacks on Shakespeare. Unlike traditional theorists, Frye means to leap the barrier between discourses: between criticism and poetry, between himself and William Blake. To do so he must tear criticism free of those very encumbrances that constitute the measure of Wimsatt's critique.

I have struggled myself with the limits of critical discourse, its conflicting fidelities to its poetic object, to theoretical procedure, and to its own nature. And I respond, if only fleetingly, to the impulse to throw over all but the last of these fidelities in an autotelic defiance. But every critic has always had to concern himself with that in poetry which makes it more than mere transcriber of the world even as it retains the need to reflect the world. His criticism, a part of the sublunary world, has had to creep along in its circumspect way and yet to soar; to share the common world of nonpoetic language and yet to ape—however feebly—the sublime world of the poet's tongue. In its long history, the circumspect practice of criticism has hardly led to theoretical resolutions that leave us with the satisfactions of a final revelation. Its failures may be seen as reflecting this fallen world's gaps, its yawning discontinuities. Which of us has not wished to rise to a total vision of our task? Those won over by Frye indicate the risk some of us would run in hope of such a vision. As circumspect critics and theorists bound to this world, the others of us, after our long history, cannot point to such success as to allow us to reject Frye's radically alternative procedure with much assurance—even if our circumspect habits force us to worry about what we must view as theoretical irresponsibility fully licensed and theoretically urged.

Every critic, then, whether before or after Frye, has had to find in poetry some kind of mediation between sublunary nature and the high seriousness of its own lunar world. Every critic should respond with sympathy to Frye's reading of the close of *The Tempest* with its rebirth of innocence and Eden. The genial artist-magician has given substance to his vision in the world: "out of the cycle of time in ordinary nature we have reached a paradise . . . where spring and autumn exist together." "When Prospero's work is done, and there is nothing left to see, the vision of the brave new world becomes the world itself, and the dance of vanishing spirits a revel that has no end." [12]

No wonder Frye sees *The Tempest* as clearly his play. So I find it appropriate to conclude with figures borrowed from it. In what has preceded I have tried to account for the resistance to the flightiness, the unearthly irresponsibility of the poet—and the critic after him—as Ariel. But we must remember that the stub-

[12] *A Natural Perspective: The Development of Shakespearean Comedy and Romance* (New York, 1965), pp. 158-59.

born earthly pull can lead downward to the poet and critic as Caliban, who in his earthbound darkness worshiped false gods. Clearly any critic or poet should prefer to be master of both Ariel and Caliban, Prospero, dedicated to the world, but to the world so transformed aesthetically, so commodious, so fit for human habitation, that he can abjure the magic that was the agent of this transformation. Here indeed would be a marriage between the poet-critic's heaven and our hell, the marriage that Frye has radically sought to perform.

# Northrop Frye

\*

## *Letter to the English Institute*
## 1965

I AM very appreciative of the great honor done me by the English Institute, and my absence is due to a proper sense of it. I should want the discussion, in particular, to be as uninhibited as possible, which it can only be if the *corpus delicti* is not, like Finnegan, able to obtrude on the proceedings. I have no itch to demonstrate that my views are "right" and that those who disagree with me are "wrong," but my presence would almost force me into some such role, to the great detriment of free speech. Nor do I wish to correct others for "misunderstanding my position": I dislike and distrust what is generally implied in the word "position." Language is the dwelling-house of being, according to Heidegger, but no writer who is not completely paranoid wants his house to be either a fortress or a prison.

I thoroughly approve of the Institute's policy in devoting a group to the study of a contemporary critic, and I can think of

one reason why I may be a good critic to choose. Every critic
tries to be coherent and consistent, and to avoid contradicting
himself. Thus he develops his insight into literature out of a
systematic framework of ideas about it. But some are better at
concealing this framework than others, especially those who are
unconscious of it, and so conceal it from themselves. I have been
quite unable to conceal it, hence the question of the systematic
nature of criticism itself bulks prominently in my writing. On the
first page of the *Anatomy* I tried to explain that the system was
there for the sake of the insights it contained: the insights were
not there for the sake of the system. I put this on the first page
because I thought that that page was more likely to be read than
others. In spite of this, I am often regarded as a critic equipped
with a *summa critica* who approaches all his readers much as
Jonah's whale approached Jonah. Actually I am grateful to be
read on any terms, but the role of system and schema in my
work has another kind of importance. Whatever the light it
throws on literature, it throws a good deal of light on me in the
act of criticizing. It is the schematic thinker, not the introspective
thinker, who most fully reveals his mind in process, and so most
clearly illustrates how he arrives at his conclusions.

I think that criticism as a whole is a systematic subject. But
I do not think that the criticism of the future will all be contained within the critical system set out in my books. Still less
do I think that it will be contained in an eclectic system, a tutti-
frutti collection of the best ideas of the best critics. One of the
most accurately drawn characters in drama is Reuben the Recon-
ciler, who is listed in the *dramatis personae* of Ben Jonson's *Sad
Shepherd,* and whose role was apparently to set everybody right

at the end. Jonson never finished the play, so he never appeared. I wish we could throw away the notion of "reconciling," and use instead some such conception as "interpenetration." Literature itself is not a field of conflicting arguments but of interpenetrating visions. I suspect that this is true even of philosophy, where the place of argument seems more functional. The irrefutable philosopher is not the one who cannot be refuted, but the one who is still there after he has been refuted. This is the principle on which I base my view of value-judgments in criticism. I have never said that there were no literary values or that critics should never make value-judgments: what I have said is that literary values are not *established* by critical value-judgments. Every work of literature establishes its own value; in the past, much critical energy has been wasted in trying to reject or minimize these values. But all genuine literature, including Shakespeare, kept turning up, like the neurotic return of a ghost, to haunt and perplex the criticism that rejected it. I think criticism becomes more sensible when it realizes that it has nothing to do with rejection, only with recognition. To recognize is of the gods, as Euripides says. In criticism, as in philosophy, argument is functional, and there is bound to be disagreement. But disagreement is one thing, rejection is another, and critics have no more business rejecting each other than they have rejecting literature. The genuine critic works out his own views of literature while realizing that there are also a great number of other views, actual and possible, which are neither reconcilable nor irreconcilable with his own. They interpenetrate with him, and he with them, each a monad as full of windows as a Park Avenue building.

I think that this argument also describes the atmosphere and pervading attitudes of the English Institute as I have experienced it: candid, receptive, courteous, and individualized. It is a pleasure as well as an honor to entrust my own work to its judgment.

ANGUS FLETCHER

*

*Utopian History*
*& the* Anatomy of Criticism

L I K E Georges-Eugène Haussmann, Préfet de la Seine under
Napoleon III, Northrop Frye has cleared a "dense confusion of
houses in the center of the city" to create broad, unbroken avenues
from one neighborhood to another. His *Anatomy of Criticism* is
utopian city planning. Its creation of large boulevards "will permit the circulation not only of air and light but also of troops";
its penetrating lines "will lead travellers straight to the centers
of commerce and pleasure, and will prevent delay, congestion,
and accidents. . . . Thus by an ingenious combination the lot
of the people will be improved, and they will be rendered less
disposed to revolt."[1]

Critics often fight undeclared wars, and any theorist who would
free the traffic of criticism must harmonize variant and even

[1] Prospectus quoted in Sigfried Giedion, *Space, Time and Architecture*
(Cambridge, Mass., 1952), pp. 535–37.

discordant interests. Like Baron Haussmann he must deal with a city that has grown more or less at random in response to historical accident. City planning frequently begins when it is too late; one asks, is it too expensive to rebuild? Furthermore, theoretical networks like the *Anatomy* are always called "antihistorical," since they openly resist the uncontrolled evolution of historically changing cityscape, on which they impose a simpler, reductive, more efficient system of intercommunication. They replace narrow alleys and byways with cold impersonal "cannonshot" boulevards. Many a fine and private place must go to make way for the new metropolis. The young delight in this new scene, as we find is the case with Frye, whose influence on the younger scholars is not at all, as some aver, the magic of scholastic nomenclature, typological exegesis, numerological cabala; on the contrary, what appeals to the younger scholars in Frye is the openness of his system, the freedom with which he catapults himself and his readers from one *arrondissement* to another. But does this freedom do violence to history, does it threaten a loss of the intimate past, the familiar, the biographical, the unique event in literary evolution?

In recent years philosophers have studied the forms of history with renewed vigor.[2] Some have asked whether history displays any valid general laws, others whether historical inevitability is defensible, still others whether a more limited determinism does

[2] For example: Patrick Gardiner, *The Nature of Historical Explanation* (Oxford, 1952); William Dray, *Laws and Explanation in History* (Oxford, 1957); W. H. Walsh, *Philosophy of History* (rev. ed., London, 1958); Morton White, *Foundations of Historical Knowledge* (New York, 1965); Arthur C. Danto, *Analytical Philosophy of History* (Cambridge, 1965).

not govern the course of events. Analytic philosophy has stressed the narrative element in history, arguing that by narration the historian "explains" the past. This latter view conflicts most sharply with the tendency of "speculative" or "philosophical" history to explain the past by describing the "philosophical shapes of history." One such shape would be Spengler's tragic pattern of cultural decline, and this sort of ideal schema is broadly opposed by analytic philosophy. On the other hand, a distinguished historian of ideas, Frank Manuel, has recently said: "The urge to place himself in a total time sequence—the real impetus to philosophical history—seems to have possessed Western man for more than two thousand years, and it is probably stronger in our culture than in most others we know." [3] This empirical observation is beginning to have a special relevance to the present, when several thinkers speak, paradoxically, of an "historiography of the future." [4] Prediction on a large scale is a sort of pre-scribed history. Utopian or social-planning in its drive, it departs radically from the traditional format of chronicle. Of this variant on philosophical history the analytic philosophers would say also that it is properly speaking not history, but a kind of theology or prophecy. Such is the debated context in which we must question Frye's historiography, since it appears partially to be history of the future, but retains elements of traditional chronicle. The *Anatomy* combines multiple techniques and outlooks.

[3] Frank E. Manuel, *Shapes of Philosophical History* (Stanford, 1965), p. 137.

[4] E.g., Bertrand de Jouvenel, *L'Art de la Conjecture* (Monaco, 1965); Daniel Bell, *The End of Ideology* (New York, 1962); Harrison Brown, *The Challenge of Man's Future* (New York, 1954).

Various critics have held that an unresolved conflict between Frye's theory of archetypes and the fluid texture of history weakens the *Anatomy* irreparably. My aim in this paper is to meet this objection and to show that it misses the point of Frye's theoretical method, which is, in a positive sense, utopian. If, however, the theoretical center of the *Anatomy* (Essay III) is a structure of unhistorical ideas, if we interpret its Polemical Introduction as an antihistorical prologue, and if finally we regard the historical theory of Essay I as too schematic or rigid to allow for actual human history, we shall have accused the *Anatomy* of irrelevance and inequity. On the other hand, there is considerable disagreement among philosophers and historians as to what history is, so that to defend Frye against the charge of inequity we need only show that the *Anatomy* and its extrapolations, the later occasional essays and lectures, have taken full account of history in some intelligible and acceptable way. We shall find that historical observations are basic to the *Anatomy* and further that a type of utopian historiography is the special method Frye employs to connect his visions of the past and future. We shall first have to see how history permeates the *Anatomy,* and then examine his special historiographic method.

The treatise begins with an essay entitled "Historical Criticism: Theory of Modes," and from this platform are launched all the subsequent arguments of the book. Essay I discerns in our literary past two cycles of five periods each, and these five successive periods are described as five distinguishable literary "modes." The term "mode" is appropriate because in each of the five the hero is a protagonist with a given strength relative to his world, and as such each hero—whether mythic, romantic, high mimetic, low mimetic, or ironic—is a *modulor* for verbal architectonics; man is the measure, the *modus,* of myth. Since "in literary fictions the plot consists of somebody doing something," and most fictions have plots of some kind, heroes and the heroic modality are an invariant element in the history of literature (so that Thackeray makes a special case of his "novel without a hero"); but as stronger or weaker than other heroes, each particular hero is a variable in history. Essay I traces a system for weighing each hero's relative power, measured in a context provided, not by the actual world, but by his own fiction. "The somebody, if an individual, is the hero, and the something he does or fails to do is what he can do, or could have done, on the level of the postulates made about him by the author and the consequent expectation of the audience." [5] By accenting the importance of the audience in this complex equation, we can describe hypothetical relations between the literary work and the real world in which its author created it.

Essay II, "Ethical Criticism: Theory of Symbols," shows how given historical perspectives favor certain attitudes toward symbol —for example, how copyright law affects our ideas about literary convention and the borrowing of archetypal motifs. The literal, descriptive, formal, archetypal, and anagogical phases of symbolism have historical parallels with the five modes of Essay I. Modern ironic literature abounds in a conventionalized literalism, descriptive symbolism provides the language of low mimetic novels, formal symbolism that of high mimetic Renaissance and neoclassical poetry. Archetype and anagogy are the symbolic matrices of romance and myth, respectively. Here the historical scheme of

[5] *Anatomy of Criticism* (Princeton, 1957), p. 33.

Essay I, which covers immense time-spans, can be implemented on the level of textural analysis, where the unit of criticism is the image, the symbol, the literal sense of the word, and so on. Essay II yields a microscopic method for determining the truth of Essay I by looking at the changing hero's symbolic accoutrements. It tends to examine literature as if it were frozen into thematic units, whereas Essay I keeps the hero before us and draws atten- tion to the kinetic aspects of poetry.

Essay III, "Archetypal Criticism: Theory of Myths," shows how myths and archetypal conventions undergo historical transforma- tion. To indicate their dynamics, Frye analyzes them for their moments of reversal, recognition, climax, and so on, moments where the audience experiences a "transfer of imaginative en- ergy." [6] Although we can isolate archetypal heroes as symbols, these heroes never exist outside of stories of some kind. Stories validate their existence and inevitably archetypal analysis makes a kind of motion study. Thus the Oedipus myth is an archetypal detective story, which modulates in *Hamlet,* retaining its struc- ture of detection. Myths do not encapsulate heroes and heroines, except with extreme allegory; they reveal them acting, and a stress on recognition as the coordinated perception of theme $+$ story (*dianoia* [7] $+$ *mythos*), which we find throughout Frye, implies that some movement, some literary dynamism, has already been experienced by the reader before reaching the moment of recogni- tion.

The experience of the reader, however, does not define the archetype. Rather the archetypal elements are likely to remain

[6] *The Educated Imagination* (Bloomington, 1964), p. 129.
[7] See *Anatomy,* p. 365, on extension of Aristotelian *dianoia.*

hidden to the reader, though working on him. Only the critic, or the reader as critic, will perceive these "structural principles," which like those of a building will be hidden to the average person, but apparent to the architect. As a structural principle any myth **may** exist skeletally, by itself—the fairy tale version of Cinderella; or can be engineered into a more complex genre—the Cinderella story of Rossini's opera *La Cenerentola;* or may even become a special substructure of a seemingly alien design—the Cordelia story in *King Lear.* What carries over from one occasion to another is the structural properties of the story, which are, since myth *is* story, those of a certain rhythm. Predictably, Frye often compares literature and music in order to stress the fundamentally rhythmic nature of the former.

The history of literature, its remembered past, is then said to include three sequences of parallel developments: the hero modulates through five modes, symbolism through five phases, and myths through these five modes and phases together (since "myth" is accompanied by archetypal imagery and symbol). History is the medium in which these changes of the unchanging occur, the medium of civilization. Its quality is not easy to describe, but on all three levels the constants of literature metamorphose gradually under cultural pressure. Hero, symbol, and myth are fundamentals of an artistic process, and these three elements remain elemental even as they undergo phenomenal change. Their triple modulation is the complex process to which Frye has given the notably Freudian name of "displacement." To the extent that this term has kept its psychoanalytic meaning, it denotes the distortions which an idea or a desire will undergo when put under pressure from a censor of some kind. Displacements alter the imagery of dreams, disguising our instinctual drives, but they never extinguish these drives, so that the psychoanalyst can read back from the distorted, displaced imagery and mythmaking to the archetypal original (which in classical psychoanalysis is often a childhood original). Displacement in the meantime has enabled the original drive to get into consciousness, if only in disguise. Generally Frye uses displacement to mean all the devices by which a myth, which would otherwise now be strange, uncanny, or somehow unbelievable, becomes plausible, "credible, logically motivated or morally acceptable" [8] to a given audience. This is basically a developmental theory of mythopoeia. Its bias is to stress the ways in which particular cultural styles impress changes upon given myths until their primary forms are sometimes hard to discern under the modern disguise. The later work of Joyce would be an apt testing ground for the theory. As an historian the critic shows, for example, the integration of Homeric myth and Viconian myth into Joyce's modern, ironic fictions. As philologist he treats the highly evolved language of *Ulysses* and *Finnegan's Wake,* to show how these works literally displace earlier linguistic forms. The power of these techniques proves the usefulness of the concept of displacement, whose orientation toward the dynamics of change, which undoubtedly it derives from its Freudian original, enables the critic to write a continuous, living history of the poetic act.

Nor is the analysis of heroic, symbolic, and mythic displacement the only way in which Frye would employ historical techniques. Whereas in tracing the broad, historical patterns of hero, symbol,

[8] "Myth, Fiction, and Displacement," *Fables of Identity: Studies in Poetic Mythology* (New York, 1963), p. 36.

and myth, the critic is focusing on the work of literature itself, on its internal properties, he can also mediate between the work and its audience, to indicate how each work is slanted in such a way as to meet a particular occasion. Newspaper critics perform this labor every day, advising audiences on the likelihood of getting their money's worth at the box office, or at the bookstore. On a loftier plane the historian will study the relations between an ancient work and its audience, hoping to recapture the original conditions under which the work was produced, partly out of simple curiosity, but also because he believes that by knowing these conditions we can reproduce the work for ourselves in a style more closely approaching the "original intention." However uncertain may be the pursuit of intention, it seems a reasonable pursuit.[9] Both journalist and historian share a technique for recapturing intention—rhetorical analysis—and despite some sharp complaints in the Introduction, the *Anatomy* gives a major place to this analytic in its fourth essay.

"Rhetorical Criticism: Theory of Genres" would doubtless provide a test case for judging whether a critic makes stock responses within his own field. Frye as always keeps what is useful from the received opinions about genre; he invents only where there is a lack of terms. But the governing concept of Essay IV is the radical one of *rhythm*—each genre has its own distinguishing rhythm, and the term is understood to mean something both large and small in scale. Thus, the large rhythm of epic and the novel is continuous flow, and this on a smaller scale can be studied as

[9] See W. K. Wimsatt, "The Intentional Fallacy," *The Verbal Icon* (2d Noonday ed., New York, 1960), pp. 10–14; and, in the same volume, "History and Criticism: A Problematic Relationship," p. 265.

the effect of the line and phrase-unit, i.e., prosodically. Frye has been much criticized for oversimplifying prosodic problems, but I suspect that this criticism only shows an ignorance of the median level of generality at which the *Anatomy* examines all its objects. It does not account for intricate variations of prosody as it does not account for similar variations in myth or imagery. It does tell us where to look and what to keep in mind when we look. It sends us into open vistas. In Essay IV it tells us that whatever else we do as generic critics we must keep in mind that genre, as experienced, is always rhythmic experience.

Scansion, meter, movement, and kinesthetic experience involve the passage of time in literature, a subject which needs to be approached on an increasingly microscopic level of analysis. Yet such analysis ought in principle to be associated with a similar, but macroscopic analysis of literature in time. Any divorce between the two would seem unsystematic. Thus the fourth essay places generic criticism under the heading of Rhetoric. Rhetorical criticism shows how a work is presented to its audience, by what devices a given fiction persuades a given audience, which usually means, gets it to attend. Such an approach is therefore concerned with particular historical periods and transitions, because devices of persuasion are aimed at man as a creature of the moment, as a creature with money in his pocket. Rhetorical devices are stylings, stylizations, decorations, fashionings, and mannerisms whose equivalent in the field of costume indicates clearly enough that we are dealing with historical change when we deal with genre. Indeed the most changeable aspect of literature is style, and style —the term—implies the minute description of genre. Stylistic critics are the experts of generic microstructure and naturally spend much time analyzing the nervous system of the literary public, the delicate mechanisms of taste, as for example we find with both Auerbach and Spitzer. With the latter, style led directly to considerations of *stimmung, milieu,* while Auerbach's essays include studies of social context (*la cour et la ville*), the reading public of late antiquity and the early Middle Ages, the controlling influence of historical fact upon the typology of the *Divine Comedy.* By contrast it might be held that Frye has never, even in *Fearful Symmetry,* done justice to style. The point is debatable, and although by standing back from poems he bars himself from close textural analysis, he has a way of quoting passages that point directly to whatever is stylistically crucial, or pointing to climactic moments where style is felt willy-nilly. Finally, of course, the point is well made: Frye is not a stylistic critic. He is a thematic critic and a theoretician of literature and criticism, and what counts is not only that he has a place for style and genre but more important that his emphasis on movement and rhythm brings style and genre together under a rhetorical theory of symbolic action. Rhetoric so understood is bound to be historical in its frame of reference, as Frye himself has shown in his brief introductory essays on Byron, Yeats, and Dickinson.

History then is a factor in Essay IV not only because tastes outside of literature, e.g., a taste for Byronic behavior, change and intertwine with our own shifting lives and these in turn force writers to meet their audiences halfway if they are to meet at the box office at all, but because the microscopic aspect of genre, namely style, is the most socially responsive of literary phenomena. Furthermore, stylistic variations depend upon elements less fusible, which Frye locates in the realm of archetypal story-form, since without some such unchanging ground bass you cannot build the habit of stylistic response. Stylistic criticism ends up as a sort of moral criticism, which engages ideas of character, and those critics most openly concerned with morality will often base their comments on rigorous textual reading, for instance the "modal" histories of Josephine Miles, or on sensitive impressions of style, of which many of Erich Auerbach's essays would be an instance. In the *Anatomy* the morality of style is reflected in the fact that "ethical" criticism (Essay II) is concerned with imagery and poetic language, the ornamental means by which poetical structures become poetical textures. Symbol in general is ethical because it is polysemous; its ambiguities fit the actual world. The hypothetical world of symbol-making and symbolic action is a social world, a world in which, as we communicate, we make a community. When we are speaking on a literal level we simply take the community as it is; our words fit the established usage with the minimum of metaphoric turbulence. But as we employ allegories, myths, anagogic visions, we begin to change that network of communication. We change its language, for one thing, but we also change its ideas and sense of itself. Our metaphors and visions enlarge the community through a power we still commonly call "imagination." The high point of the Theory of Symbols is the outlining of archetypal and anagogic vision, and these are systems of imagery in which human civility and love are mirrored. Thus "in its archetypal aspect, art is a part of civilization, and civilization we defined as the process of making a human form out of nature. The shape of this human form is revealed by civilization itself as it develops; its major components are the city, the garden, the farm, the sheepfold, and the like, as well as human society itself. An archetypal symbol is usually a natural object with a human meaning, and it forms part of the critical view of art as a civilized product, a vision of the goals of human work." [10] Civilization may be defined in any number of ways, but none could avoid a factor of temporal development, so here again the central mythic symbols are by definition tied into the developmental history of mankind. It is hard to see how such a system denies the essential value and significance of history, as some critics have implied.

The higher plane of anagogy is only the imagery of whatever is imaginably more benign than civilization itself, which I suppose must, in a phrase, be the exercise of love. The polymorphous nature of love pure and unconfined needs a place in critical theory: "In the anagogic phase, literature imitates the total dream of man. . . . anagogically, then, poetry unites total ritual, or unlimited social action, with total dream, or unlimited individual thought." [11] What distinguishes Frye from other visionaries is the way in which he unites these two realms.

Ritual action and dream vision can unite, plausibly, because the governing concept of unity is "the goals of human work." Elsewhere Frye makes the telling comment that "everything man does that's worth doing is some kind of construction, and the imagination is the constructive power of the mind set free to work on pure construction, construction for its own sake. The units don't have to be words; they can be numbers or tones or colors or bricks or pieces of marble. It is hardly possible to un-

[10] *Anatomy,* pp. 112–13; also pp. 141 ff.      [11] *Anatomy,* pp. 119–20.

derstand what the imagination is doing with words without seeing how it operates with some of these other units." [12] To believe
that construction is the main exercise of the imagination seems to
me markedly right for a theory of Western literature. We can
think of literary "making" in numerous ways, but perhaps the
commonest are the two which bound the *Anatomy*. Genre is the
traditional shape-making of this craft. The hero is the central,
defining figure of these traditionally evolved generic forms.

Essay I is of course our chief document in assessing the historiography of this "pure construction." It maintains that we can
"classify fictions, not morally, but by the hero's power of action,
which may be greater than ours, less, or roughly the same." [13]
This gives us five discernible levels of relative power, ranging
from a mythical upper limit where the hero is a god, down
through romance, high and low mimetic modes, until at the
lower limit we reach heroes who are "inferior in power or intelligence to ourselves, so that we have a sense of looking down
on a scene of bondage, frustration, or absurdity," this last being
the ironic mode. Our heroes become gradually weaker as the
postclassical cycle of European literary history unrolls. "We can
see," says Frye, "that European fiction, during the last fifteen
centuries, has steadily moved its center of gravity down the list.
In the premedieval period literature is closely attached to Christian, late Classical, Celtic, or Teutonic myths." [14] And the cycle
which begins around the year A.D. 500 ends with the modern
phase where the typical hero is a Joseph K. or Winston Smith.

[12] *The Educated Imagination*, pp. 119–20.      [13] *Anatomy*, p. 33.
[14] *Anatomy*, p. 34.

Frye notes that "something of the same progression may be traced in Classical literature too, in a greatly foreshortened form."

This historical schema has obvious precedents. Vico had periodized cultural growth in cycles. Frye himself notes the Spenglerian shape of his cyclical theory: "The containing form of historical criticism may well be some quasi-organic rhythm of cultural aging." [15] The shift from one mode to another is conceived as a continuous process, with a tendency for poets to hark back to their "modal grandfathers," to the mode before the one immediately preceding their own. Sometimes, special sensibilities inspire change in the displaced hero—so that, for example, from an unfortunate traveler he may modulate into a sentimental traveler or a sentimental stay-at-home—and then history looks more dialectical in its main outlines. According to this view, in the words of René Wellek, "sudden revolutionary changes, reversals, into opposites, annulments and, simultaneously, preservations constitute the dynamics of history." [16] By contrast the theory of Essay I scarcely resembles a Darwinian theory of literary evolution, because even though the long stretch of poetic tradition seems unified through time, this art "does not evolve or improve: it produces the classic or model." [17] Instead the imaginative progress of literature is no progress at all; it is a fulfillment of the potentialities of its classical models. Finally the most general precedent for Essay I is the attempt of various critics (not all of them literary) to

[15] *Anatomy,* p. 343.

[16] "Evolution in Literary History," *Concepts of Criticism* (New Haven, 1963), p. 40.

[17] *Anatomy,* p. 344.

define historical periods.[18] Each mode is in a sense a period whose length is determined by the predominance of a literary norm, the hero. Each mode is also "periodic" in that it makes a cycle capable of recurrence, unlike a unique duration of time, wherever that might be discerned.

One plausible view of Essay I is that it employs a kind of idealist metaphysic: this history is the chronicle of the chief stages in the evolution of the idea of the hero. Each hero is a sort of world-historical man—but there is less commitment here to inevitability than one might at first expect. In any event this essay should, in a complete analysis, be measured against the Hegelian statement that "World History exhibits the development of the consciousness of freedom on the part of the Spirit, and of the consequent realization of that freedom," [19] if only because the fivefold decline in heroic freedom and power might seem to proceed in opposite directions from that statement. No matter how the concept of Spirit (*Geist*) is interpreted, Hegel asserts that some sort of freedom is "realized." Similarly, various other philosophies of history have suggested that man progresses slowly toward a triumphant liberation of self through technological, scientific, philosophic, or theological improvements, and these systems will have to confront the apparently correct judgment that the heroes of the major works of the last fourteen hundred years have, in general, become progressively weaker. The Hegelian scheme at least has the merit

[18] On periodization, see Wellek, *Concepts of Criticism,* pp. 92–93, 199 ff.: also, Wellek and Austin Warren, *Theory of Literature* (New York, 1952), pp. 252–60; Steven Marcus, "The Limits of Literary History," *New York Review of Books,* II, No. 4, 10–11.

[19] As quoted in Walsh, *Philosophy of History,* p. 143.

of pointing to spirit, which, transferred to the poetic realm, is imagination, a power the poet exercises in the increasingly liberal perception that man as a social or political being has become gradually less free. The imagination governs whatever the poet creates and adorns in the fictive world, and since literature is free creation its history need not be written up as a variety of economic, social, political, or even religious activity. If poetry were no more free than history, then the gradual weakening of Western man as an actual agent of an actual life would reappear, directly reported, in literature, and the frustration of modern man would be directly shared by the frustrated modern poet. But not only must actual life be distinguished from art, as so many have insisted for so long, but even the "existential projections" of art must also be thus distinguished.[20] Art, which is neither a copy of life nor a psychic projection onto life, enjoys the privileges of games being made up by players as they play the game; it derives, but is distinct from, actual human existence. The freedom of the creative imagination is of this game-playing order.[21]

Literature presents us with images and stories—the *Anatomy* treats them as hypothetical models—of human life. They are like those free versions which are subtitled *"after* Baudelaire," *"after* Villon." Tracing their history, we cannot avoid a riddle which has hardly been solved or even correctly posed, namely the problem of mimesis. If literature presents us with heroes who are "imitations," what is the process of their imitation? When the Greeks

---

[20] See *Anatomy,* pp. 63–65, 139, 211.

[21] Not merely as described in Johan Huizinga, *Homo Ludens* (Boston, 1955; orig. ed., 1938), ch. vii; cf. Freud's paper, "The Relation of the Poet to Day-Dreaming (1908)," *Collected Papers* (London, 1950), IV, 173–84.

held that poetry was a mimetic art, they took for granted that pictures of things exist and can be made, but this is so common in our experience that we rarely ask how it comes about. Modern critics at least know that mimesis and representation are not easily defined in simple visual terms. To mime is not to photograph, which could never have been known before the invention of photography, except that painting approximates photography through devices of *trompe l'oeil,* on which even Aristotle comments favorably.

Miming is a conversion of reality which is not an exact duplication of "something out there." It is by no means easy to show philosophically what is meant by the phrase "the same as," or "looks like," and the problem is not solved by saying that in principle one should be able to imitate reality by duplicating it. Plato had early seen that mimesis involved participation and almost something like eating up the objects of imitation. The gap between duplication and mimetic representation seems hard to measure, but it exists—our experience of photography tells us so. Auerbach's *Mimesis* attempts the measurement of the process by an indirect analysis in terms of language, syntax, and "levels of style," the classical theory of decorum to which *The Well-Tempered Critic* recently drew attention again.

Everything in Frye, and much in other critics, including Auerbach, suggests that an adequate definition of mimesis will depend on an idea of poetic rhythm. The different genres typically have different sorts of hero (or antihero) and they project him, according to the *Anatomy,* through the microscopic establishment of particular movements of style. Perhaps the history of literature is finally the history of changing aesthetic responses to changing environments, and the main property of this response is a kinesthetic one, the capacity to participate in actions. Aristotle's stress on action is a stress, inevitably, on rhythm, and when the scope of literary history enlarges beyond the period covered by the *Poetics,* it takes the shape of an epic struggle for imaginative freedom.

The freedom of the poet must be distinguished from that of his creations. The heroes of myth are stronger and freer than those of irony, but Hesiod is hardly more free than Swift or Kafka. Imaginative freedom seems to remain a constant, expressing itself in varying ways. Speaking of the way Blake saw the optimistic evolution of "a world-wide commercial unity . . . emerging from national rivalries," Frye says, "It is difficult to see how art can evolve in a similar way, for the quality of art never improves. But it may increase in conscious awareness of the implications of vision as the work of a growing body of predecessors accumulates and is, however, haphazardly, preserved. Milton is not a better poet than Sophocles because he follows him in time, but his ability to use Sophocles may have given him a more explicit understanding of what his own imagination saw." [22] I would call this growth of conscious awareness an increase in the capacity to respond, which, however, accompanies a progressively darkening view of man's heroic capabilities. The movements of the fictive and real worlds seem to cancel each other out, leaving imagination a constant. Perhaps Lord Acton, were he to have written the famous history of liberty, would have shown us all the elements of the dialectic Frye invokes in his first essay, all those many ways in which a man may be free or enslaved, a poet

[22] *Fearful Symmetry* (Princeton, 1947), pp. 260–61.

free or enslaved, his hero free or enslaved. Certainly the decline
of individual freedom seems strange enough, when contrasted
with man's obviously broadening control over his physical environment.

The poetic theory of William Blake, to which Frye owes so
much, may suggest one reason why this enlarged control does
not evoke a mimesis of increased freedom (except when the poet
is a propagandist). Blake teaches lessons of political liberty, but in
his late prophetic poems these lessons transcend common political
forms. The center of Blakean libertarianism is a rich sense of the
human body, of its profane sanctity, a sacred unity of body and
mind whose medium is the imagination. This imagined unity is
the natural matrix of poetry, its chosen vessel. But modern life
has seen what might be called a general loss or clouding of the
body-image. In advanced technocracies the human body is in need
of exercise; less and less active—the idea of poetic "action" is
at once affected—it becomes the passive cargo of increasingly
dominant vehicles. Further, what once were tools and extensions
of the human body now become extensions of machines only.
Machines today can manufacture machines. The human touch
disappears in simple physical ways, at least for *homo faber*. Traditionally poetry has shown a primitivist tendency to explore the
self in its natural habitat, the body, or in other terms to explore
the limits of the self, one of which is the body. No more eloquent
testimony to this centrally poetic act could be instanced than the
works of Kafka, where the body is everything; he is the chief
modernist of the imagination. Modern man may deny his mortality and bodily form, but literature will not, and literary criticism

must account for the tenacity with which poets come back always to the locus of freedom, which is surely the mind-body unity in its relation to the environment, a relation mainly determined by the short span of life.

The ironic tone of modern literature bespeaks a conflict between this mortality of man and the grandiose message that both benign and perverse ideologies broadcast to us continually, namely that we control our world more and more. History as we know it may then adequately approximate the image Frye presupposes, underlying his theory of modes. At least it will be reasonable to examine the span of Western literature to see if indeed there is not some systematic relation between the declining sequence of the five modes and the ascending sequence of technological advances Western man has actually achieved. Another approach, perhaps more profitable, will be to see if the five modes could not occur in any order, without decline, ascent, or any other positive trend.

There still remains the question as to whether such schematic diagrams will yield true insight into our *literary* past. Each of the five descending phases of literature would allow exceptions all too easily—a mixture of irony and romance, for example—and these exceptions are seemingly frequent when one looks closely at the past. Following Collingwood the practicing historian might say: "The cyclical view of history is . . . a function of the limitations of historical knowledge. Everyone who has any historical knowledge at all sees history in cycles; and those who do not know the cause think that history is really built thus. When they come to settle the exact position and rhythm of the cycles, no two exactly agree." [23] On this view panoramic divisions of the past are purely subjective, and will change with each era and with each historian: "Some system of cycles there must always be for every historical student, as every man's shadow must fall somewhere on his own landscape; but as his shadow moves with every movement he makes, so his cyclical view of history will shift and dissolve, decompose and recompose itself anew, with every advance in the historical knowledge of the individual and the race." The projected pattern—the shadow—may have either a personal or a more authoritative philosophical source. Supposing the latter were the case with Frye, his theory of history would belong to the branch of so-called speculative or philosophical historiography, where, as Isaiah Berlin puts it, "the pattern, and it alone, brings into being and causes to pass away and confers purpose, that is to say, value and meaning, on all there is. To understand is to perceive patterns." [24] The empirical and everyday historian looks for particular facts and tries to write the history of what happened, but, as Walsh remarks of Hegel's *Lectures on the Philosophy of History,* "The philosophical historian, by contrast, is struck by the fragmentary and inconsequential character of the results thus achieved, and looks for something better. This something better is the divination of the meaning and point of the whole historical process, the exhibition of reason's working in the sphere of history." [25] If the term "imagination" were substituted for "reason" in this description, these words would apply aptly to the

[23] "Theory of Historical Cycles: II," as quoted by H. Stuart Hughes, *Oswald Spengler* (New York, 1962), p. 158.

[24] *Historical Inevitability* (London, 1954), p. 14.

[25] *Philosophy of History,* pp. 142–43.

*Anatomy.* I have already remarked that Frye is neither exactly Viconian, Hegelian, evolutionary, cyclical, or any other completely speculative sort of historian, though he takes ideas from all these. Of necessity he recombines materials, because the history of imagination is a yet unexplored field. He is, for example, cautious about claiming that the last cycle of irony turns back upward toward myth or romance. Essay I can be described as a prolegomena to a more meticulous periodization of literary history, and it remains deliberately rough, without giving up the hope that each mimetic phase could be distinguished and analyzed in great detail. The theocentric bias of medieval thought could be closely handled, to test its bearing on romance; the courtly cult of the prince in the Renaissance could be related to the methods of high mimetic; the rationalism of modern science to the canons of low mimetic; and so on, through much subtler inquiries than these. In principle there is no reason why Essay I could not form the basis for a freely conducted practical investigation of historical fact.

The true difficulty in thinking about Essay I lies elsewhere. Unfortunately not even historians of politics and economics are fully agreed as to what history is. Although much philosophical attention has been given to this matter, most statements about it, if they are general, will remain controversial. Historians are not clear as to what are their data. Are they events? If so, what or how long is an event? Are they explainable events? If so, what is historical explanation? These are not new questions: they were raised by Thucydides, by Augustine, by the historians of the Romantic period, by positivists, and most recently by analytic philosophers.

Analytic philosophy, by looking at the language of history writing, has made it possible for recent authors to present one very helpful notion, that history "explains" the past by presenting a story of it, or of a part of it. Rather than promulgating historical laws (if they exist), the historian writes narratives, something which indeed was taken for granted by all earlier practitioners of the art. Narratives in history "are used to explain changes, and, most characteristically, large-scale changes taking place, sometimes, over periods of time vast in relationship to single human lives. It is the job of history to reveal to us these changes, to organize the past into temporal wholes, and to explain these changes at the same time as they tell what happened—albeit with the aid of the sort of temporal perspective linguistically reflected in narrative sentences." [26] Such sentences refer to events in the past, and do not pretend, in this case, to depict or forecast the future. The narrator cannot speak prophetically without violating the main limits upon his knowledge, its pastness and its unfinishedness. But, by accepting the former limit fully, the narrator can give accounts of change—since that is what stories are—and the crucial part of the story, in this respect, is neither its beginning nor its end, but its middle, where the changes occur. (Compare such organic story-forms with stories where change occurs at the end only, since usually the latter require the conventional use of a *deus ex machina* or some other apocalypse.) The explanatory section of the history of Oedipus, for instance, is the middle of *Oedipus Rex,* that section of the play which has something both before and after it, that section which we invoke when we seek to explain Oedipus' plight to ourselves, as he sought to explain it to himself.

[26] Danto, *Analytical Philosophy of History,* p. 255.

On this basis Essay I is history proper (as opposed to some sort of speculative theory of history only), because it tells a story. Its tale is rough and abruptly told. Within each of the five modal periods it locates a castle of identity, a central manner of presenting the hero, and as each period gives way to its successor, as each castle falls, the essay records the narrative of a decline. The middle of the story as a whole is the triumph, in two cultures, ours and the Greco-Roman, of the high and low mimetic modes —the whole therefore constituting a tragic drama of the fall of these modes. We can say that this is the kind of story or drama an author would make if he regarded Western literature from a sufficient distance away from its particular data. Looked at from a distance, what other stories are possible? No doubt several, but their theme would not be the presentation of the hero. Yet they too would explain our imaginative past. Curiously, Erich Auerbach, who looked closely at literary products, was not able to write an epic of mimesis. He wrote strings of episodic incidents, and such was bound to happen, given his short distance from his object.

A longer range tends to allow detachment of the critic from the canons of any particular modal period. Frye has consistently attacked our own "ironic provincialism, which looks everywhere in literature for complete objectivity, suspension of moral judgments, concentration on pure verbal craftsmanship, and similar virtues,"[27] but there are other forms of historical bias, and all are equally destructive when they become rigid ideologies.

A practicing literary historian might feel inclined to call Frye's scheme of the past "unreal." When one enters a historical period

[27] *Anatomy,* p. 62.

and looks about at the scattered remains, the endless minutiae
which at least since the invention of printing have been available
for study, one cannot help wondering if schematic histories do
justice to the disorderly past. Everyday historians, working in-
ductively, do not want to gain their detachment at the price of
losing palpable realities. And yet they too must give a shape to
their mass of data, so that even when they do not write what
Frye, following F. H. Underhill, calls "metahistory," their works
must have an informing pattern of some kind. The historian,
Frye says, "works toward his unifying form, as the poet works
from it. . . . In a sense the historical is the opposite of the mythical, and to tell a historian that what gives shape to his book is a
myth would sound to him vaguely insulting." [28] When a historian
frankly admits that *mythos* or plot does govern his selection of
detail, he is admitting to a form of thought which is only partly
inductive, and is much more largely theoretical and universaliz-
ing in its drive to make sense of the past. Such is the metahistory
of Essay I; it is no less a type of history for combining induction
and deduction.

Nor is the schema of Essay I a rigid formulation. Though it
centers on heroic fiction, it allows theme to be central and the
heroic peripheral, whenever the poet speaks to us discursively or
didactically, when in his *persona* the poet becomes the hero of
his own work. Essay I allows for tragic and comic variations,
naïve and sentimental phases, in which the heroic and thematic
plots can be represented. It places several standard terms for period in their relations to the fivefold image of history. In general
it avoids the paratactic order of mere chronicle. The essay as a

[28] "New Directions from Old," *Fables of Identity,* p. 55.

whole presents a hierarchy of ideas. On its lowest level it treats the history of Western fiction in an almost fictional way, which I have called its tragic drama; on a second level it explains history by structuring it into a story, whose coherence is a large part of its meaning; but finally, it does correspond to the past in some way, and judges history in the light of certain alleged historical facts concerning the hero. This last correspondence to actual fact is the most problematic of the three levels, and to assess its adequacy we must consider the genre of its expression.

The *Anatomy,* like every essay in criticism, needs to be accorded the privileges of its own natural rhythm, which is that of the genre, anatomy. Viewing it as such, we can fix its intentions. With some irony Frye's fourth essay describes the generic properties of this "extroverted and intellectual" form.[29] Frequently satiric, intellectually and thematically slanted, full of lists and diagrams, encyclopedic in sweep, anatomies "rely on the free play of intellectual fancy and the kind of humorous observation that produces caricature." The genre descends from Menippean satire and "differs also from picaresque form, which has the novel's interest in the actual structure of society. At its most concentrated the Menippean satire presents us with a vision of the world in terms of a single intellectual pattern. The intellectual structure built up from the story makes for violent dislocations in the customary logic of narrative though the appearance of carelessness that results reflects only the carelessness of the reader or his tendency to judge by a novel-centered conception of fiction." This could be the portrait of the *Anatomy,* whose single intellectual drive is to argue for a theoretical whole body of literature and

[29] *Anatomy,* pp. 308–14.

literary language. Evidently the genre assumes wholeness and hence becomes encyclopedic, but within this wholeness it cuts out endless fragments, whose coherence is a given of the argument and whose correspondence with historical reality will be based on a kind of humorous observation.

Anatomy is useful to literary theory and more narrowly to literary history, because it can take the form of a utopia. Frye himself has noted the utopian nature of many anatomies; one suspects that because of its drive toward a single pattern anatomy is the genre in which utopian ideas are most readily expressed. In general utopias present "an imaginative vision of the *telos* or end at which social life aims." [30] By analogy the *Anatomy* would present a vision of the end toward which criticism tends, especially if criticism is conceived as a socially complex enterprise. Frye is concerned with the present and future of criticism—of utopias he remarks that they usually project their vision into the future or into some faraway place—and one essential critical function (yet to be accomplished) is the analysis of our literary past. The breezy, high-speed spinning of patterns and themes in the four essays creates a discursive form not unlike that of the great English model of this genre, Burton's *Anatomy of Melancholy*, but Frye may be more deeply influenced by More's *Utopia*. This should not be taken to mean that he has abdicated a conceptual standpoint for a fictional game; rather he has adopted a mode of expressing (frequently through metonymy) theoretical relations which are those, as we said, of an immensely complicated city-planning design. (In the range of his interests he is remarkably like Paul Goodman, author of the pioneering *Structure of Literature, Communitas, The Empire City,* and *Utopian Essays and*

[30] "Varieties of Literary Utopias," *Daedalus,* Spring, 1965, p. 323.

*Practical Proposals.*) The traditional model for utopia is an idealized city, the classical *polis* of Plato's *Republic,* and the question raised by Frye's utopian intentions is whether this political model will describe our critical "society" adequately, with sufficient detail to demonstrate the openings available to the lively modern critic.

For one thing the utopian *polis* may be restrictive in its spatiality. As the mass of information and printed matter increases in the world, criticism theoretically occupies more and more space; but another way of putting this new situation, which we experience every time we enter a university library, would be to say that the simultaneity of critical expressions continually increases, because although thought itself may be as slow and painful as ever, the reproduction and publication of thought has speeded up, while more and more scholars are at work to accelerate this process even further. There is now too much information to be simultaneously processed or shared, and yet our assumption strengthens every day that somehow scholars should attempt to share and assimilate this mass of data. The human machine of the scholarly community is itself a utopian conception,[31] but its potentially unlimited productive power has rather resulted in a kind of universal scholarly flux, where no fixed locus of opinion

[31] In "Utopia, the City and the Machine," *Daedalus,* Spring, 1965, pp. 282–86, Lewis Mumford argues that the ancient city was itself a utopian construct in its original format, which broke down into a *dystopia, a kakotopia.* The city was in either case a "collective human machine, the platonic model of all later machines. . . . The reason that this machine so long evaded detection is that, though extremely complicated, it was composed almost entirely of human parts. Fortunately the original model has been handed on intact through a historic institution that is still with us: the army."

seems possible. Frye has observed of utopias in general that "if there is to be any revival of utopian imagination in the near future, it cannot return to the old-style spatial utopias. New utopias would have to derive their form from the shifting and dissolving movement of society that is gradually replacing the fixed locations of life. . . . A fixed location in space is 'there,' and 'there' is the only answer to the spatial question 'where?' Utopia, in fact and in etymology, is not a place; and when the society it seeks to transcend is everywhere, it can only fit into what is left, the invisible non-spatial point in the center of space. The question 'Where is utopia?' is the same as the question 'Where is nowhere?' and the only answer to that question is 'here.'"[32] These remarks refer to political utopias, but I think they apply a fortiori to our literary world.

The "here" of literary criticism is the mind of the critic, which contains such shifting, multifarious knowledge that it amounts to a "non-spatial point in the center of space," a nowhere. The *Anatomy of Criticism* is indeed its author's own mental anatomy and presents his thoughts as a single intellectual pattern. More exactly this is a Blakean mind informed by mythopoeic prophecy, as Frye has confessed in several places. The information explosion has so restructured the idea of what fundamental data are that now, unless we imagine these data as all "equally alive, equally parts of the same infinite body which is at once the body of God and of risen man,"[33] or as some similar conceptual unity, we are not likely to make much further sense of our critical profession, except perhaps by withdrawing into extreme privacy. As writers

[32] "Varieties of Literary Utopias," p. 347.
[33] See *Anatomy*, pp. 118–22, 141–46; *Fearful Symmetry, passim,* but especially pp. 423–28, on the "anagogical" in poetry.

have frequently said in recent decades that they write only for small, select audiences, so critics may create an elite for which their work is alone intended. But then, in a yet narrower way, the withdrawn critic would belong only to another smaller utopia, the Oneida County of his own private thoughts. Expansion of information has cosmically altered our situation. It has enforced a cosmic utopia upon us, both as a fact of our thinking and as a purpose preferable to the elitist criticism which is an obvious alternative. As De Jouvenel has said, we should try to manipulate the "coefficients of common fate" toward a greater *individual* freedom.[34] Planning may seem dangerous to freedom, but lack of planning is yet more dangerous. The *Anatomy* in part recalls the old-fashioned utopias of the *polis,* and displays a variety of diagrammatic street-planning which is clearly spatial. On the other hand, its insistence on the Blakean body of total vision which is literature is an attempt to say that space, geometrical space, does not and cannot define the temporal flux of the critic's full literary experience. By stressing body Frye stresses movement and the unimportance of diagrammatic fixity in the utopian plan. The total form is necessarily more like a cloud than a house; its network of interrelated sections is always changing in design. In fact the excitement of utopian speculation at present is a consequence of rejecting the older spatial plan and the admission of change as an essential quality of stable theory. The city of today can only plan for a stable tomorrow by thinking of the day after tomorrow.

Normally we do plan for the future, and the use of utopian

[34] "Utopia for Practical Purposes," *Daedalus,* Spring, 1965, p. 445, where De Jouvenel is referring to an article of Donald T. Campbell in *Decisions, Values and Groups,* ed. D. Willner (Oxford and New York, 1960).

critical theory to prevent an enslavement of critics by various provincial attitudes will help to safeguard the future of criticism. Liberal education invests similarly in the future. Of course, mere anticipation of an event does not guarantee that man will compass that event to his satisfaction. Planning may lead to a constriction of purpose, the antithesis of liberality. We may call this excess "futurism," and the trick will be to keep utopian thought from becoming panicky, millenarian, and merely apocalyptic. Thus it is most important that Frye finds value in imaginative freedom, that with him myth develops and is tied to the growth of civilization. Douglas Bush, speaking generally about the so-called myth-and-symbol doctrine of which the *Anatomy* is what he calls "the Bible," has asserted that "its most general limitation is that, like the old literary history and the history of ideas, it does not contain in itself any criteria of aesthetic value," and he adds, "Of course, like literary historians and historians of ideas, myth-and-symbol critics may acquire such criteria elsewhere and use them." [35] Given our argument so far, this description seems quite unfair to the historiography of the *Anatomy*. The "elsewhere" turns out to be the evolving structure of literature itself, as revealed in the history of the hero. The futurism of Essay I achieves balance because it gathers the past into its single vision. It recognizes that our practical criticism deals largely with poems made in that past; as Frye has said, in another connection, we face the past.

The problem here is to decide in what way there can be a uto-

[35] "Literary History and Literary Criticism," in *Literary History and Literary Criticism,* ed. Leon Edel, Kenneth McKee, and William M. Gibson (New York, 1965), p. 6. Cf. similar comments by René Wellek, *Concepts of Criticism,* p. 337.

pian history of that past, since we cannot alter its form by doing something now. We cannot plan the past. The past is not an open possibility. The past is finished and done with, or so we usually think. How then can utopia, which leans forward, lean backward too, without falling apart? Indeed utopian history, looking in either direction, is hard to imagine. As one political theorist has said, "Utopia is nowhere, not only geographically, but historically as well. It exists neither in the past nor in the future." [36] On the other hand, there is some disagreement on precisely whether all utopias are genuinely transhistorical and thus "timeless." Another critic has observed that in the nineteenth century a new sort of utopian thought developed, which may be called open-ended utopianism. "Up to the nineteenth century, the utopian ideal involved the ordering of life once and for all time. By contrast, the new vision entailed a constant management of run-away historical forces: to tame the future, to know in order to predict and control, to change the world—but always in accordance with its historical destiny." [37] Frye clearly belongs to this later tradition. But since the reader of poetry faces the past, the utopian critic of poetry uses the "new vision" to illuminate the developmental significance of that actual past.

[36] Judith Shklar, "Political Theory of Utopia," *Daedalus,* Spring, 1965, p. 370; see also pp. 373–79 on the historicity of utopian thought after the French Revolution. Shklar and Manuel agree generally on the increased historicity of postclassical utopia.

[37] Frank E. Manuel, "Toward a Psychological History of Utopias," *Daedalus,* Spring, 1965, pp. 303–9. "Whereas before the nineteenth century utopias are invariably stable and ahistorical, ideals out of time, they now become dynamic and bound to a long prior historical series. They should henceforth be called euchronias—good place becomes good time."

Development in the arts may be distinguished from the improvement of a science, so that the nonimproving past of literature may be seen to reach the present and extend into the future through an endless sequence of archetypal borrowings and inventions. Of the latter let me give but one slender instance, the invention of *The Beggar's Opera* by John Gay. As Johnson says of him, "We owe to Gay the ballad opera; a mode of comedy which at first was supposed to delight only by its novelty, but has now by the experience of half a century been found so well accommodated to the disposition of a popular audience, that it is likely to keep long possession of the stage. Whether this new drama was the product of judgment or of luck, the praise of it must be given to the inventor; and there are many writers read with more reverence, to whom such merit of originality cannot be attributed." [38] The progress of the ballad opera demonstrates, in lieu of other instances, that the past is by no means finished and done with. As a treaty signed in 1920 can have repercussions in 1930 and again, by displacement, in 1960, so a particular poem or generic or mythic invention may affect later poetry at some distant remove. Suppose we were to ask if the plays of Agathon are truly nonexistent, since they are not to be found on any printed page; we might counter this view by showing that they exist as some inner hidden counterpoint within the extant plays of his contemporaries, Sophocles, Euripides, and Aristophanes. We cannot easily find out if something of Agathon lives in these works, but we might—as utopians—entertain the possibility. The utopian sensitizes himself to detect elements of change which, without some

[38] In the *Life of Gay*, in *Prefaces, Biographical and Critical, to the Works of the English Poets* (1779–81).

notion of the total interpenetration of all literary vision, would remain elusive. The utopian historian searches out mere "traces" of the thoughts and acts of men, and by picking up these vestiges and ghosts of thought, hovering over his sources, this "ludic" historian tries to get time into his scheme of things, without making an unreal abstraction out of the Past.[39] On the one hand a critic like Frye, I suspect, is more sensitive to hints of the true course of events, as revealed by delicate verbal traces, than most formal historians of literature, and on the other he prefers a curiously nonlinear account of that course of events. The pretense of the formal historian is that he writes a linear account of things as they happened. Frye does not make this pretense. He asserts that what we *know about* the past is the units, the periods, by which we measure its linear movement.[40]

His essay "Varieties of Literary Utopias" has provided a preliminary model for this timeless presentation of time:

The procedure of constructing a utopia produces two literary qualities which are typical, almost invariable, in the genre. In the first place, the behavior of society is described *ritually*. A ritual is a significant social act, and the utopia-writer is concerned only with the typical actions which are significant of those social elements he is stressing. . . . In the second place, rituals are apparently irrational acts which become *rational* when their significance is explained. In such utopias the guide [previously called "a sort of Intourist guide"] ex-

[39] Thus G. J. Renier, *History: Its Purpose and Method* (London, 1950; paperback ed., New York, 1965), pp. 96–105. Renier makes the same assumption as the analytic philosophers, that history is "nothing but a story," developing this idea at length.

[40] See *Anatomy*, pp. 346–50, on the essential function of the repeated, archetypal, imaginative elements which lift works of art "clear of the bondage of history"—not clear of history entirely, but only of its tyranny.

plains the structure of the society and thereby the significance of the
behavior being observed. Hence, the behavior of society is presented
as rationally motivated. It is a common objection to utopias that they
present human nature as governed more by reason than it is or can
be. But this rational emphasis, again, is the result of using certain
literary conventions. The utopian romance does not present society
as governed by reason; it presents it as governed by ritual habit, or
prescribed social behavior, which is explained rationally.[41]

History on this plan will present the image of changes of ritual
behaviors or, in another formulation, literary behavior as a function of ritual habit. The term "ritual" points to the solution of
our problem, which was to keep time in a timeless system. Rituals
are cyclical actions, movements which are repeated, recur regu-
larly, are more stable and in a way more readily measurable, than
actions which take place "through time," where the observer is
in the unhappy position of having to keep moving in order to
keep watching the object of study (the difference between watching a moving train and watching a rotating wheel). In a sense
these circular motions of the ritual act are perfect, since they com-
bine both stillness and movement. But their perfection is less
interesting than their necessity for the calendrical division of any
linear history. To develop a measured image of literary tradition
which extends through time, we need periodic divisions of that
temporal transit. Common history calls these units "years,"
"months," "days," "hours," and "seconds," and common history
takes its cyclical units from extrahuman standard conditions (the
astral universe). Literary history can and does do the same, for
its chronological correspondence to common history. But the no-

[41] In *Daedalus*, Spring, 1965, p. 324.

tion of a literary period (and probably of other kinds of periods also) seems to require a more pliable standard than that given by the astral universe. The consequence of taking a utopian view of history is that a basic periodicity of creation as a ritual act is made available to the historian. In creating the hero and his story, the poet "is concerned not with what happened but with what happens. His subject-matter is the kind of thing that does happen, in other words the typical or recurring element in action. There is thus a close analogy between the poet's subject-matter and those significant actions that men engage in simply because they are typical and recurring, the actions that we call rituals." [42] Since the imitation of ritual is myth, the creation of the hero, his imitation, inevitably employs the repetition of archetypes and their displaced equivalents. Human experience, conceived periodically, is time informed by ritual recurrence. A period of literary history is a linear duration of literary activity viewed as a cyclical process. The main task for theoretical history is then to determine what are the chief literary rituals.

Essay I asserts that one of these, perhaps the cardinal ritual, is the recurrent creation of the hero. Each of the five phases is a theoretical time-unit, defined in terms of an attitude toward the hero. If Frye actually thought that any given cycle (e.g., that of high mimetic) had an a priori temporal duration—as we might consider the durations of the day and night given to us by the rotation of the earth around its own axis—his theory would be chimerical. But he has defined utopian life as a combination of ritual and habit where the two are rationalized through their quality of recurrence. There is no linear time *in* the time-units we

[42] Frye, "New Directions from Old," *Fables of Identity,* p. 53.

use, and there is no linear time *in* the cyclical phase-units of Essay I. Such secular time is (if anything) a property of life that is merely measured by such units; the units are not synonymous with that life, but only measure it, as a ten-yard gain in a football game is one thing, the measuring chain another. There is indeed no reason for the historical cycles to have the feel of linear time in them; they have, in a way, no feel at all, since they are only measures. And yet they do have a normal relevance to the excitements of life, with all its accidental surprises, because they are derived from an observation of the over-all quality of that life, namely that with surprise it combines recurrent events. They are especially useful because they measure linear time as fulfillment. Here Frye may be thought again to follow Blake. "Everything that has ever happened since the beginning of time is part, Blake says, of the literal Word of God. The ordinary historical conception of human existence as a dissolving flux in linear time is therefore the literal approach to life, the corporeal understanding based on memory. History as the total form of all genuine efforts of human culture and civilization is the canon or Scripture of human life. History as linear time is the great apocrypha or mystery which has to be rejected from it." [43] Only by developing a sensible unit of duration can this Scripture be recorded, which explains why the *Anatomy* takes its measure of time from that most palpable entity, the hero.

The main difference between an imaginative cycle, a cycle of ritual poetic habit, and the rotation of a wheel is that the former is plastic and rubbery, like the human life-cycle, where longevity is a variable. This should not imply that imaginative cycles are

[43] *Fearful Symmetry,* p. 340.

useless measures. However imprecise such units may seem, when compared with the divisions of time measured by the hand of a watch, they are still the bare necessity of any account of the imaginative periodicity of literature. If we want linear history without corruption, we must settle for its problematic fullness, which is not so much a plethora of facts (though that makes a difference) as it is a complexity of feeling and thought and action which defines each genuine era in terms of a single, almost musical sound-pattern. Listening to any symphonic piece, we are not always aware of the merging of complex waves that constitutes this unified sound. The unity of an era is a matter of unified feeling tone; there is a certain aura about life in the "age of x or y," and only by trying to measure this elusive constitution of waves will the historian become something more philosophical than a bibliographer. In practice the most exciting and most readily revealing way to study the wave form of a cultural period is to analyze moments when it appears to change into a new wave form. These moments have been called "ages of sensibility," periods when writers cooperate with history, as it were, by focusing on the literary process instead of on the received forms of the literary product. A writer like Sterne turns the epic tradition inside out, to make his *Tristram Shandy* an experiment in the rhythm of continuity, by dislocating, twisting, liberating the syntactic forms in which long stories of epic heroes are usually told. Such authors are radically self-conscious, but in practice this means that they attend more consciously than usual to the rhythms which constitute the moving structure of literary process. Consciousness of "self" turns out to be something rather special for the writer; it becomes consciousness of the way myths and symbols and heroes

normally move. It may be no accident that the freest age of
sensibility we know of occurs near the beginning of the chief
modern political revolutions. In several essays since the publication of the *Anatomy* Frye has concentrated on this modern climate of change.[44]

Erich Auerbach began his last foray into the history of Western
letters by commenting on the extreme difficulty of attaining to
any synthetic historical view of his subject. "Enormous amounts
of material have been made available, resulting in hundreds of
specialized disciplines, most of them quite unheard of in Vico's
time, each concerned with some very partial aspect of the European problem. No one can possibly master all these branches of
study." [45] Nor is it likely that a polymath, were he gifted with
immense factual knowledge, could synthesize simply by piling up
historical particulars, since in itself synthesis means order and
pattern, a transcendence of the mass. Auerbach therefore pre-
ferred a philological method of "point of departure," typically a
pregnant phrase like *la cour et la ville,* from which he could
trace lines of significant literary and social development. He
sought contexts for poetic forms and believed that these forms
were significant only when they were placed against recaptured,
supposedly unique historical contexts. To perform this feat required the most imaginative choice of "point of departure" so
that each would allow the maximum radiation of meaning with

[44] "Towards Defining an Age of Sensibility," "The Imaginative and the
Imaginary," "Yeats and the Language of Symbolism," all in *Fables of Identity.*
[45] *Literary Language and Its Public in Late Latin Antiquity and in the
Middle Ages,* tr. by Ralph Manheim (New York, 1965), p. 17.

a maximum of philological control. Usually this meant choice of a stylistic element, since style could be controlled by the history of language, while it could be given general, even universal human relevance through its connection with decorum and the entertainment of particular audiences. Auerbach, in short, worked mainly within the confines of the critical discipline outlined in Essays II and IV of the *Anatomy,* and he invoked history in the manner we have already associated with those essays.

Rhetorical and stylistic analyses allow the most close-up views of poetry, and it is possible that a critic who gives himself to microscopic study can never happily assume a more distant perspective on his subject. Auerbach wrote history in the Viconian tradition, bringing the past into the present by linguistic comparisons, through the biography of the language poets use. His opposite number will be the critic who watches the evolution of thematic forms. A convivial critic like Frye, who has avowed that his early sympathies were with the *Odyssey* rather than the *Iliad,* who styles himself an "Odyssey critic," will be at home in the comic middle distance of critical response. The very tendency toward theory which everywhere determines Frye's work is a sign that he needs no help in remembering the mass of existing literary documents, which as he says "are far better worth reading than any history of them could ever be." From this Homeric, Odyssean belief in the value of experience arises an abstract countercurrent, which in both the *Odyssey* and the *Anatomy* takes on the rhythm of utopia. Both works seem at first to follow an overdetermined, single line of action; both works end by having defined a circle. As Frye has said of a particular literary history, their effect is to "reawaken and refresh our imaginative experience by showing what unexplored riches of it lie within a certain area." [46]

The utopian style plays hand in hand with the humorous observation and realism of both the Homeric poem and its critical, anatomic descendant, the *Anatomy.* A critic chiefly responsive to that sort of poem is a primarily comic, romantic, and theoretical person whose main interest is the special untruth of poetry. Odysseus specializes in telling tales which are implicit commentaries on the whole idea of telling tales, and this is very much Frye's style. Generic and generous, this style may be contrasted with the "high seriousness" of the *Iliad,* whose subject is wrath and tragedy, whose fiction attempts a close correspondence with physical reality. The low seriousness of the *Odyssey* permeates the *Anatomy,* which explores the coherence and the means and modes of travel between different sections of the critical world. Truth and untruth in this context become mainly relative, as truth in the *Odyssey* became relativistic through the displacement of the hero. By such explorations the critic hopes to achieve a sense of unity in disorder, as if the world of criticism were a wondrous Mediterranean basin.

Finally history in the *Anatomy* appears to restore "sacred time" to the domain of criticism.[47] For the mere profanity, secularism, thingness, and progressivism of the purely linear historian, Frye would seek to enlist a mixed methodology, where that

[46] Review of Bonamy Dobrée, *English Literature in the Early Eighteenth Century,* in *The Griffin* (August, 1960).

[47] See Mircea Eliade, *The Myth of the Eternal Return* (New York, 1954), *passim;* also Eliade, *The Sacred and the Profane: The Nature of Religion* (New York, 1959), ch. ii, "Sacred Time and Myths"; and *The History of Religions: Essays in Methodology* ed. M. Eliade and J. M. Kitagawa (Chicago, 1962), especially the essays by Daniélou, Eliade, and Heiler.

linear history is combined with the ritual periodization of the poet's imaginings. "Sacred time" is the opposite of mere futurism, with its perverse millenarian zeal. The futurist (and here of course I do not mean the Futurist school of art), though he uses the terminology of historical cycles, does not believe in the human actuality of these cycles; almost the opposite is true for him—his "ages of man" are empty fields. He wants to stop time, rather than bring any period of it to fulfillment, and he wants to get off the world. By exaggerating the linearity of history he can bring it to catastrophe, to a sudden, explosive, final end. Antithetically, by introducing "sacred time" into linear history, the critic accepts all regular, recurrent, traditional, inherited goods. His criticism is, in a precise sense, periodic, festive, memorial, and dancelike. Man as a creature and creator of the imaginative period is free within controls, a musical being. His movements within fiction correspond not so much to the things of nature as the rhythms of nature—one perceives the provincialism of *this* critical view, a eurythmic rapture—and through his own originality he imposes variation on the forms derived from those rhythms. By reminding us of man as a breathing, walking, eating, copulating, as well as thinking, loving creature, Frye's periodic history testifies to fundamental qualities of life itself. I have called this "dancelike," I might have said "graceful." The imagination resists dictation, and the history of literature must be the chronicle of that rebellion. Under the circumstances, when information is expanding both present and past so rapidly before our eyes and the future is moving toward us at an accelerating rate, which encourages catastrophic thought, it seems natural and useful to employ utopian, periodic forms to outline the history of imaginative freedom.

# W. K. WIMSATT

*

## Northrop Frye: Criticism as Myth

> poetry must wait on fact.
> And we have seen that when the hero lifts
> The vizor of his helmet to the gaze
> Of the ecstatic myth-mad populace
> . . . it is nothing but a shell, a voice
> Without a face. . . .
>
> —Karl Shapiro, *Essay on Rime,*
> III.4.1937–42

> Not all critical statements or procedures
> can be equally valid.
>
> —Northrop Frye, "Literature as Context: Milton's *Lycidas*,"
> *Fables of Identity*, p. 128

IN ACCEPTING the mandate of our chairman to write and deliver this paper, I have been told that this is a program set up in honor of our subject, and that, though I am expected to be critical, "searching," even skeptical, I must be so "respectfully," that is, I must bear in mind the honor of the occasion. As I always write respectfully of literary theorists, I do not find this stipulation irksome. I think I have written in its spirit. I would add the reflection that, as the devil's advocate is not called in until the prospect of canonization is imminent, and furthermore as it is extraordinary that such proceedings should take place at all during the lifetime of the candidate, I believe the honor of the occasion can be in little danger.

The rapidly expanding volume of Frye's writing in the vein of Gnostic mythopoeia, as well as his many but elusively varied repetitions and his paradoxes, create for the critic of Frye an expository problem at least as difficult as the argumentative.

According to Frye, primitive man (somewhat like any person we can imagine beginning life on a desert island) begins by wishing the world were a more comfortable place, that is, more "like" human nature. He enacts certain rituals to try to make it that way. And also he tells himself certain metaphoric and analogical stories embodying his assimilative wishes, and when these wishes project a shape of heroic divinity, investing the natural environment, we have in the proper sense "myth." [1] There is one basic and inclusive myth, which takes the shape of a divine quest, death, and rebirth, following the cycle of the four seasons. Out of myth evolve literature and its very important primitive "conventions," with differences from original myth that may not be fully clear. In literature metaphoric imagination replaces the magic of ritual.[2] Yet literature demands of us, if we are in tune, a "primitive response." [3] Myth and literature do not imitate nature. Having begun apparently with some uneasy glances at nature, they go their own way, madly, transcending, absorbing,

[1] "Myths are stories about divine beings which are abstract and stylized stories in the sense that they are unaffected by canons of realism or probability" ("Blake after Two Centuries" [1957], *Fables of Identity: Studies in Poetic Mythology* [New York, 1963], p. 141).

[2] *A Natural Perspective: The Development of Shakespearean Comedy and Romance* (New York, 1965), pp. 59–60, 116, 146.

[3] *A Natural Perspective,* pp. 61, 64.

enveloping. So that the singing school is not the world (from the world poets have nothing to learn), but literature itself. Literature is made out of earlier literature. It develops into one master, apocalyptic structure, a "universal human form," the heights of heaven and the depths of hell.[4] It includes all partial constructions of myth anybody might conceive, no matter how ambitious—the White Goddess, the Hero with a Thousand Faces.[5] (The phrase "Myth of the Eternal Return" would appear to be another name for the same central ideas—ritual, repetition, divine archetype.) Man, if he has enough imagination, lives not in the supposed "real" world of "nature" but in and by this dream structure of "pure un-inhibited" wish-fulfillment and of obsessive anxiety.[6] It is important for young people to be educated into this structure, and this is done by the reading of the greatest bodies of myth, the Bible (which is total but vague) and the Greek and Roman classics (which are clear but fragmentary).[7] In some broader way, all the efforts of our verbal wisdom—philosophy, history, science, religion, law—are myths, all myths, that is, imaginative constructs. The actual ruling myths of the past have all proved illusory. Literary study helps us to see through false myths, half-truths, mob speech, and gabble idioms. It helps us, above all, to conceive the permanent myth, that which is not illusory, not imaginary, but imaginative, the vision

[4] *The Educated Imagination* (Bloomington, 1964), p. 42; *The Well-Tempered Critic* (Bloomington, 1963), p. 155: "The universe in human form"; "The Realistic Oriole: A Study of Wallace Stevens" (1957), *Fables of Identity*, pp. 250–51.

[5] *The Educated Imagination*, pp. 20–21.

[6] *The Educated Imagination*, p. 43.

[7] *The Educated Imagination*, pp. 46–47.

of the possible ideal "real" world, the "real form of human society"—the "free, classless, and urbane society"—"hidden behind the one we see." [8] "Nature" in this apocalypse gets itself "inside the mind of an infinite man who builds his cities out of the Milky Way." [9]

Let me introduce here a brief bibliographical note. In this account of Frye's system, rude, but I believe fundamentally faithful and correct, I have been reflecting the organon of 1957 (*Anatomy of Criticism*). But the dimensions and some of my phrases are taken from more recent works and especially from the series of six CBC lectures published in 1963 as *The Educated Imagination*. This is Frye's best attempt to write a small-scale account of his system. Another set of lectures, delivered at the University of Virginia, and published, also in 1963, as *The Well-Tempered Critic,* begins with capriccio variations on the ancient theme of high, low, and middle styles, and on verbal rhythms, but ends with some instructive repetitions of central ideas. Other pregnant statements are to be found among sixteen of Frye's shorter essays collected under the title *Fables of Identity* in the same year, 1963. In that year appeared too his Evergreen Pilot Book *T. S. Eliot.* And in that year he delivered at Columbia University the lectures published in 1965 as *A Natural Perspective;* these deal with primitive conventional patterns in Shakespearean comedy and romance.

---

[8] *Anatomy of Criticism* (Princeton, 1957), pp. 115, 349; *The Educated Imagination,* pp. 44, 60–67; "The Archetypes of Literature" (1951), *Fables of Identity,* p. 18: ". . . the central myth of art must be the vision of the end of social effort, the innocent world of fulfilled desires, the free human society"; and "The Imaginative and the Imaginary" (1962), *Fables,* p. 167.

[9] *Anatomy,* p. 119.

Let me now continue my exposition and begin my argument with Frye by quoting two authors in whose classic thought Frye finds several of his own starting points—Plato and Aristotle. Plato, in the *Ion* (540 B–C), where the rhapsode is quizzed to the point of saying that a rhapsode (that is, a literary critic) will know the right things (*ha prepei*) for a man to say, the right things for a woman, for a slave, or for a freeman—but not what the slave, if he is a cowherd, ought to say to his cows, or what the woman, if she is a spinning-woman, ought to say about the working of wool. And Aristotle in chapter IX of the *Poetics,* where in general he says that poetry is more philosophic and of graver import than history, and in chapter XXV, where he says that, if a poet utters technical inaccuracies about the pace of a horse or about medicine or any other art, the error is not essential to the poetry; and if he does not know that a doe has no horns, this is less serious than if he portrays the doe "inartistically," "indistinctly," "unimitatively," or "unrecognizably"—*amimētos.* No translation of this adverb makes very good sense, because with this word Aristotle is touching a tender spot in the mind of criticism. He is defining a circle of paradox (or contradiction) within which literary theory has ever since that time continued to move—and Frye no less than any other thinker who makes a serious effort to explain the difficulty. I mean the double diffi- culty, of poetry in relation to the world, and of criticism in rela- tion to value—the so-far irreducible critical experiences: that literature is both more lively and less lifelike than the real world (this impossible pig of a world); that criticism cannot demon- strate value but is at the same time inescapably concerned with trying to do so. Frye is in no different situation from Aristotle,

Coleridge, Croce, or Richards, in having to confront these experiences and in being unsuccessful in trying to simplify them. In his thinking on these problems Frye differs from other literary theorists mainly in the extreme assurance, the magisterial sweep and energy, with which he at moments attempts (or pretends) to detach literature from the world of reality, and criticism from evaluation, and in the aplomb with which he involves himself in the oddities, implausibilities, even patent contradictions, required for this detachment. Thus, literature, on the one hand, has no reference to life, it is autonomous, like mathematics, and sufficient to itself; it "takes over" life, envelops and absorbs it,[10] swallows it.[11] Literature is made out of other literature.[12] At the

[10] *Anatomy*, pp. 122, 349, 350.

[11] Cf. *The Well-Tempered Critic*, pp. 149, 154–55; *The Educated Imagination*, pp. 33, 35: "literature as unlike life as possible." In "Nature and Homer" (1938), *Fables of Identity*, p. 41, the view is attributed to Aristotle and Longinus. The same essay, pp. 46–47, contains Frye's most resolute attempt to argue that literature is altogether allusive and verbal. It is "not externally or incidentally allusive, but substantially and integrally so." Apparent returns from convention to experience are only shifts to a different convention. Cf. *The Educated Imagination*, p. 16; and "Literature as Context: Milton's *Lycidas*" (1959), *Fables of Identity*, p. 125, on Wordsworth and ballad conventions; *Anatomy*, p. 122: "literature existing in its own universe . . . containing life and reality in a system of verbal relationships." See also Frye's *Selected Poetry and Prose of William Blake* (Modern Library, 1953), p. xxvii: "Suppose we could think away the external or nonhuman world: what would the shape of things be like then? Clearly the whole universe would then have the shape of a single infinite human body. Everything that we call 'real' in nature would then be inside the body and mind of this human being, just as in a dream the world of suppressed desire is all inside the mind of the dreamer."

[12] *The Educated Imagination*, pp. 28–29: ". . . there's nothing new in literature that isn't the old reshaped . . . . there is really no such thing as

same time literature does refer to life, it must; [13] it began with real life in a primitive situation, and it is concerned with promoting values for real life, the vision of the ideal society (unless we mean that this is only a dream—as perhaps we do—but then why all the talk about the difference between the genuine and the phoney?).[14] *Lincoln Wasn't There* is the title of a recent well-conceived spoof on the ritual theory of mythic origins. If we were to judge by numerous passages in Frye, we'd have to conclude that the ocean wasn't there either, the wine-dark ocean that washed the shores of Greece, nor the rosy-fingered dawn, nor the pine-clad mountains. Nothing was there but the blind bard himself, the *words* of some earlier ballads, and an audience, which presumably did not include any ox-eyed or white-armed women, or any men who were crafty, sulky, proud, brave, or cowardly.

In his Polemical Introduction of 1957, Frye is intent on purging criticism of several wrong kinds of valuing, the biographical or genetic, the rhetorical, the moralistic, and the socially prejudiced.

---

self-expression in literature. . . . We relate . . . poems and plays and novels . . . to each other"; and pp. 15–16: "A writer's desire to write can only have come from previous experience of literature . . . . literature can only draw its forms from itself"; and *The Well-Tempered Critic,* p. 147.

[13] See, e.g., *The Educated Imagination,* p. 25: "There's always some literary reason for using them, and that means something in human life that they [sheep, flowers] correspond to or represent or resemble." Cf. *The Well-Tempered Critic,* p. 148. And see Meyer Abrams, "The Correspondent Breeze," in *English Romantic Poets* (New York, 1960), p. 49, an excellent passage on "the inescapable conditions of the human endowment and of its physical milieu."

[14] Cf. "The Imaginative and the Imaginary" (1962), *Fables of Identity,* pp. 152–53: "Sense . . . tells us what kind of reality the imagination must found itself on."

Like Arnold in 1880, he wishes to distinguish such exercises of
mere locally public taste from judgments of "positive value,"[15]
which he says are the proper business of criticism. He can and
is willing to distinguish "ephemeral rubbish,"[16] mediocre works,
random and peripheral experience,[17] from the greatest classics,
the profound masterpieces, in which may be discerned the con-
verging patterns of the primitive formulas. At other moments,
however, he says that criticism has nothing whatever to do with
either the experience or the judging of literature. The direct
experience of literature is *central* to criticism, yet somehow this
center is excluded from it.[18] Criticism moves toward an undis-
criminating catholicity of "interest."[19] The patterns of the 1957
Introduction have approximately repeated themselves in later
pronouncements. On a single page of a statement in an MLA
pamphlet of 1963 on *Aims and Methods of Scholarship,* "good
taste" and "value-judgment" are said to be based on direct experience; at the same time "good taste" is a skill founded on a
structure of knowledge, and this knowledge (or at least an important part of it) is academic criticism, and critics who go wrong
usually do so, *"not* through the failure of taste and judgment, *but*
through not knowing enough about literature."[20] On one page
of *The Well-Tempered Critic* the "study" and "understanding"

---

[15] *Anatomy,* p. 27.      [16] *Anatomy,* p. 116.      [17] *Anatomy,* p. 17.

[18] *Anatomy,* pp. 20, 27, 28. Let us make a collection of banknotes and
then proceed to use them as stage money, or a collection of ten-dollar gold-
pieces and then treat them as subway tokens.

[19] *Anatomy,* p. 24.

[20] *The Aims and Methods of Scholarship in Modern Languages and
Literatures,* ed. James E. Thorpe (New York, 1963), p. 62. The italics are
mine.

of literature are "different things" from the "admiration" of it and the "wonder," but on the next page we hear of the "fallacy of separating the understanding of literature from the appreciation of it." [21] In his MLA pamphlet statement of 1963 and also in a lecture published in *College English* for October, 1964, Frye thinks critics ought to avoid the risk of working from their own likes and dislikes and keep a business eye open to their reputations and their effectiveness. Critics who attack Milton only damage their own images. In the latter essay, "good" and "bad" become "not something inherent in literary works themselves," but qualities of activity or passivity in our own "use" of literature, so that evaluative criticism itself is no longer to be directed toward literature but toward earlier bad criticism.[22] Frye is a candidate for the votes of all shades of appreciators and scientists in criticism —except that of the unhappy analyst who finds himself under obligation to make comparisons. His key terminology and his most

[21] *The Well-Tempered Critic,* pp. 136–37. ". . . there clearly are such standards [i.e., of taste]" (p. 132). ". . . both intellect and emotion are fully and simultaneously involved in all our literary experience" (p. 144).

[22] "Criticism, Visible and Invisible," *College English,* XXVI (October, 1964), 10, 12. This lecture flourishes a number of Frye's most blatant reneges and contradictions. The title is a religious metaphor. Criticism can be either "militant" or "triumphant." In the phase of triumph, "glorified and invisible," criticism is just not comprehended by darkness and ignorance.

A critic who undertakes to chart Frye's vagaries on the theme of criticism and value will suffer from an embarrassment of riches—as at least one other writer, Philip P. Hallie, in the *Partisan Review* (Fall, 1964), has illustrated with his own series of passages from the *Anatomy.* See also the review of the *Anatomy* by Meyer Abrams in the *University of Toronto Quarterly,* January, 1959, p. 192.

picturesque statements suggest some kind of neutral anatomizing, but we must remain unsure, as he no doubt is unsure, whether he wishes to discredit all critical valuing whatever, or only the wrong kinds of valuing.

What is it that enables Frye to get away with these violations of logic and order? Unquestionably, the speed and energy of his style. Let me insert here a general encomium on the liveliness, the moments of vivid wit and charm which Frye brings to the contemporary critical scene—the freedom and swash and slash with which he employs what in his lectures *The Well-Tempered Critic* he himself has so well described as the rhythm of association, the discontinuous, the aphoristic, the oracular style.[23] In *The Educated Imagination,* Frye quotes a teacher of his, Pelham Edgar, who once told him "that if the rhythm of a sentence was right, its sense could look after itself." It is true that in order to write, we must have something to say. But having something to say, adds Frye, means "having a certain potential of verbal energy."[24] Frye has learned the lesson of his teacher surpassingly well. Two other papers than the one I have written might take their departure from this point: one in praise of Frye's many brilliant theoretical, but local, insights, one in complaint against his frequently shuffling associational logic and syntax, which at the worst I would describe as a kind of verbal shell game. I have written neither of those papers, but a paper on Frye's system, which, despite one or two disclaimers on his part regarding its

---

[23] *The Well-Tempered Critic,* pp. 85, 92, 104. "Such techniques have for their object the attempt to break down or through the whole structure of verbal articulation" (p. 92). Cf. *Anatomy,* pp. 329–37.

[24] *The Educated Imagination,* p. 52.

importance,[25] is after all the most prominent feature of his writing. At the moment, I am saying that Frye has contributed much to the gaiety, the fun, and hence in a certain sense to the health of modern American criticism. He has enlivened our proceedings. For this we should be grateful. Frye's vigorously urbane recitals will start in our minds echoes of many voices in the idealist and mythopoeic tradition, from Blake to Frazer, Cornford, or Lord Raglan. But most often I find myself hearing again the masterly jokes which I read first as a boy in those dialogues of Oscar Wilde *The Decay of Lying* and *The Critic as Artist.* "Hours ago, Ernest, you asked me the use of Criticism. You might just as well have asked me the use of thought." "The elect spirits of each age, the critical and cultured spirits, will grow less and less interested in actual life, and will seek to *gain their impressions almost entirely from what Art has touched.*" "As a method, realism is a complete failure. . . . wherever we have returned to Life and Nature, our work has become vulgar, common and uninteresting." "One touch of Nature may make the whole world kin, but two touches of Nature will destroy any work of Art."

Because, of course, as Frye could have explained to Wilde, the work of art is made of other works of art, and other works of art are made of the mythic archetypes.[26] We are now in a position to undertake a more direct account of this distinguishing feature of Frye's literary theory. A number of things are to be observed.

---

[25] See, e.g., *Anatomy,* p. 29: "Whenever schematization appears in the following pages, no importance is attached to the schematic form itself."

[26] ". . . mythology merges insensibly into, and with, literature" ("Myth, Fiction, and Displacement" [1961], *Fables of Identity,* p. 33).

And first, and most momentous, that the mythic archetypes provide a set of predicates ("a specific conceptual framework"[27])
which Frye considers to be in some special and exclusive sense
proper to literary study, something scientifically reliable and self-
sealing. No dialectical leaks are possible. The mythic predicates
give us *real categories;* they are a ground of *valid comparisons.*
They are like the scientific middle terms of Aristotle's demonstra-
tive syllogisms; only Aristotle would never have found these in
literature. These and only these predicates come together progressively to build a totally coherent order of literary genres, of
conventions, and of words (or of literary experience). Hence
they provide a method of critical taxonomy.[28] Such predicates are
"centripetal" in the study of literature. All others are "centrifu-
gal,"[29] taking the student away from literature. In itself the system of mythic predicates is neutral—or maybe it is not neutral. It
may be inspected, or *perhaps* it may be inspected, sometimes better
in ephemeral popular works than in the classics.[30] It does not
provide a test of value. Or maybe it does. At least somehow it

[27] *Anatomy,* p. 6.

[28] "Literature as Context: Milton's *Lycidas"* (1959), *Fables of Identity,*
pp. 127–29: "For literature is not simply an aggregate of books and poems
and plays: it is an order of words" (p. 127); ". . . a recurring structural
principle. The short, simple, and accurate name for this principle is myth"
(p. 128). "It is part of the critic's business to show how all literary genres
are derived from the quest-myth. . . . the quest-myth will constitute the
first chapter of whatever future handbooks of criticism may be written that
will be based on enough organized critical knowledge to call themselves
'introductions' or 'outlines' and still be able to live up to their titles"
("The Archetypes of Literature" [1951], *Fables of Identity,* p. 17).

[29] "The Archetypes of Literature" (1951), *Fables of Identity.* p. 7.

[30] *Anatomy,* pp. 104, 116. But see the opposite view, pp. 17, 19, and
"The Archetypes of Literature" (1951), *Fables of Identity,* pp. 12–13.

does provide the education the critic needs in order to move with security on the floor of that unstable stock exchange of literary values which has given Frye so much amused concern.[31]

In his MLA pamphlet statement of 1963, Frye, repeating in capsule form his earlier accounts, wishes to put all remarks about the mere structure, themes, imagery, and language of poems in a class which he calls "commentary" or "allegorical" commentary. A second sort of remarks, all those that look in the direction of genre, convention, classical allusion, and myth, he distinguishes radically from the former, and he calls these latter not commentary but "identification," and this is the supreme act of criticism.[32] Similarly, in his *Nature and Homer,* of 1958, he

[31] *Anatomy,* pp. 9, 17–18. See in his "Myth, Fiction, and Displacement" (1961), the account of Arthur Miller's play *The Crucible* as having the "content" of "social hysteria," but the "form" of "purgatorial or triumphant tragedy." The latter is the element of permanence, what tends to give the play "an immense reverberating dimension of significance" (*Fables of Identity,* p. 37). A few pages earlier (p. 34) the "conventional comic form" in *Pride and Prejudice* "does not account for any of the merits of the novel." See the accounts of *Macbeth* in *The Educated Imagination,* p. 24 (". . . what a man feels like after he has gained a kingdom and lost his soul") and in *A Natural Perspective,* pp. 62–63: "It is not a play about the moral crime of murder; it is a play about the dramatically conventional crime of killing the lawful and anointed king." Take away "this mythical and conventional element . . . and Thomas Rymer himself could hardly do justice to the chaos that remains." And see *The Educated Imagination,* p. 48: "To see these resemblances in structure . . . will not, by itself, give any . . . notion why Shakespeare is better than the television movie."

[32] Cf. the model account of five stages in seeing the grave-digger scene in *Hamlet,* in "The Archetypes of Literature" (1951), *Fables of Identity,* p. 13, and the four "creative principles" of criticism (convention, genre, archetype, autonomous form) in "Literature as Context: Milton's *Lycidas"* (1959), *Fables,* p. 123.

argues that we cannot say good or bad of a literary work unless we can say *what* it is, what kind of literary work. As if one were to say, "This is a good comedy," and Frye were to answer, "Oh no, it isn't. It's a good satire in the third comic phase." In this line of thought, we are reminded forcefully of the relative proximity of Toronto to Chicago. In Frye's system, conventions and genres constantly play the role of premature ultimates. So far as I can see, Frye has never offered a shred of evidence for this kind of exclusiveness and essentialism [33]—but rather much that tells specifically against it: for instance, in his lectures on Shakespeare,[34] the primitive conventionalism which he insists is the structural basis of such unsuccessful plays as *Pericles* and *Cymbeline*. There would seem to be no reason whatever why a comic convention, a pastoral allusion, or a mythic stereotype should be considered a trace of the tough and abstruse essence and identification of literature, while a centrally structured image, a dramatized theme, or a persistent verbal technique should not be, but should be only something marginal, "easy" enough to notice, as Frye says, a mere topic of "commentary." The mythic archetypes, centering in the slain king, are Frye's King Charles's Head—"his allegorical way of expressing it"—turning up if not at the beginning, middle, and end of most of his essays, at least by the end in those instances where we begin to hope that they may have been forgotten.

[33] Frye, of course, finds occasions for explicit disavowals of every form of exclusivism. See, e.g., *Anatomy,* p. 62; *College English,* XXVI (October, 1964), 8.

[34] Hinted also in *Anatomy,* p. 117. Shakespeare in his later period was at the "bedrock" of drama.

Frye has indeed a keen and witty sense of the difficulties and insufficiencies of various other kinds of criticism (which he calls "comparative," not "positive"), the biographical kinds, the affective, impressionistic, "rhetorical," mimetic, realistic, moral, and sociological kinds. In some of his negative arguments he scores brilliant bull's-eyes. He has invented some of the most entertaining jokes I know in assault upon the wrong ways of criticizing which I myself would group under the head of the biographical or "intentional" fallacy. "There are critics who can find things in the Public Record office, and there are critics," he boasts, "who, like myself, could not find the Public Record Office." [35] It would distract us from the main issue to notice here at any length that in his MLA pamphlet statement of 1963 he becomes a renegade to such insights in the course of a headlong safety-first piety to the scholarly techniques and to the great names. He has found any kind of technical ignorance a "constant handicap." And let Milton offend his taste and judgment. Milton must have his reasons. [36]

But to return to the archetypes: One way to describe what is original in Frye is to say that it consists in an extreme and violent conjunction of schematism and concreteness; that is, on the one

[35] "Literature as Context: Milton's *Lycidas*" (1959), *Fables of Identity*, p. 128.

[36] Cf. Spenser lapsing into "muddled argument, tasteless imagery, and cacophonous doggerel" ("The Structure of Imagery in *The Faerie Queene*" [1961], *Fables of Identity*, p. 69) and "Milton's one obvious failure . . . *The Passion*" ("Literature as Context: Milton's *Lycidas*" [1959], *Fables*, p. 126).

*Anatomy*, p. 110, urges that "biography will always be a part of criticism."

hand, of abstraction, universalism, archetype, inclusive system, and on the other hand, of high coloration, detailed specificity, a wildly luxuriant growth of the flora and fauna, the constellations, of Frye's world of the imagination. Let us say a little more first about the schematism. This is something which Frye is often willing to labor. The study of literature seems to become, not knowing more and more precisely the character of each literary utterance (though we find at least token assertions of the individual and ineffable, as in the essay on Milton's *Lycidas*[37]), but just the opposite, knowing each one under the most universal aspects possible. Never mind the trees. "Everything is potentially identical with everything else."[38] *Metamorphoses* becomes *Fables of Identity*. Frye has pushed this ruthless, categorizing, assimilative, subsuming drive of his theory in various places, but in none I think with more complete self-exposure than in this toward the end of the third essay in *Anatomy of Criticism*.

In looking at a picture, we may stand close to it and analyze the details of brush work and palette knife. This corresponds roughly to the rhetorical analysis of the new critics in literature. At a little distance back, the design comes into clearer view, and we study rather the content represented: This is the best distance for realistic Dutch pictures, for example, where we are in a sense reading the picture. The further back we go, the more conscious we are of the organizing design. At a great distance from, say, a Madonna, we can see nothing but the archetype of the Madonna, a large centripetal blue mass, with a contrasting point of interest at its center. In the criticism of literature, too, we often have to "stand back" from the poem to see its archetypal organization.[39]

[37] *Fables of Identity*, p. 128.          [38] *Anatomy*, pp. 124, 136.
[39] *Anatomy*, p. 140.

Long ago, Horace told us that poems are like pictures, *ut pictura poesis,* in that some demand closer inspection, some, like murals presumably, look better at a distance. It has remained for mythopoeic criticism to tell us that we must back away from all of them, until they merge in a common formalism or "stylization" of archetypal colors and crude shapes.[40] Who really wants to see a painting that way? Perhaps a pure neo-Kantian "formalist" in art criticism—a Clive Bell or a Roger Fry. Scarcely a critic who has literary interests in the verbal art of literature.

As a matter of fact, no system of sheer abstractionism or universalism has ever commended itself for long to the world of litterateurs and critics, any more than to the world of poets. Plato's purity, such as it was, was conspicuously the frame of reference of an antipoetics. How Aristotle, countering Plato, used the concrete and rich colors of actual Greek epic and drama to give conviction and interest to *his* system of universals is a story for another day. A system does need its colors, its precious realizations, its exhibits. And so we come to the more specific side of Frye's mythopoeia, the detailed realization. We can readily enough see the reason for this contrasting side of the system. Still it is odd, and it is strained. The *idea* turns out to have not only a Greek or Latin name but a phallus, a mask, a goatskin jacket,

---

[40] *Anatomy,* p. 135. And see *The Educated Imagination,* p. 54, where literature in education has the same relation to other verbal studies (history, philosophy, social sciences, law, theology) as mathematics to physical sciences. See also "Myth, Fiction, and Displacement" (1961), *Fables of Identity,* pp. 28, 31; and "The Archetypes of Literature" (1951), *Fables,* p. 13: "This inductive movement towards the archetype is a process of backing up, as it were, from structural analysis, as we back up from a painting if we want to see the composition instead of brushwork."

a red wig, a sword, a staff, or what not. As one reviewer has remarked, Frye's *Anatomy* is "about as stripped and quintessential as the Albert Memorial." [41] "To generalize is to be an Idiot," said Blake, and he left his dictum joined in the record with the rebellious and exuberant particularity of his own art, where Adam is wrapped in the coils of the big green serpent and God has wings of brass. In his Introduction of 1957 Frye notices this opinion of Blake's and in the name of the archetypes he rejects it. His own articulations of the archetype are more true to his master—both in degree of specificity and in degree of fantasy. (Concepts can be highly colored and still in a sense seem uncontaminated by the touch of experience. The immediate illusion of external, fallen Albion can be avoided.) "Critical theory of genres," complains Frye, "is stuck precisely where Aristotle left it." [42] This, however, can be remedied, and will be—as, long since, the service for botany was performed by Linnaeus. Frye wants all the idealism, autonomy, and absoluteness of a subjective humanization but at the same time a highly concrete typology, variegated specific categories, a brimful inhabited world of Aristotelian genres, styles, and characters. Occam! thou shouldst be living at this hour! Benedetto Croce! thou shouldst be living at this hour! I am thinking of such arrangements as Frye's twenty-four overlapping divisions of the seasonal cycle of myths, or his permutations of high, middle, and low styles, complicated by the ideas of hieratic and demotic, and of verse, prose, and associative (or speech) rhythms, at primary, secondary, and tertiary levels, or the endless recital of parallel conventions, or hopeful

[41] Robert M. Adams, *Hudson Review*, X (Winter, 1957–58), 617.
[42] *Anatomy*, p. 13.

parallels, or qualifications or exceptions to parallels, among Shake-speare's comedies and romances. There is surely something of the archetype of Polonius and of the sock and buskin in that passage of Samuel Beckett's *Watt* where the eccentric householder Mr. Knott "mooches" about his rooms in varied footgear: "As for his feet, sometimes he wore on each a sock, or on the one a sock and on the other a stocking, or a boot, or a shoe, or a slipper, or a sock and boot, or sock and shoe, or a sock and slipper, or a stock-ing and boot, or a stocking and shoe, or a stocking and slipper, or nothing at all. . . . And sometimes he wore. . . ." [43]

In his moments of most nearly pure archetypal abstraction, Frye's types are in a sense true patterns. But in that sense they are also truistic, simplistic, and uninteresting. More or less universally valid patterns of imagery and shapes of stories can of course be discerned in the canon of the world's literature. Fictional stories, it is true, are all about what we wish to have or to be and what we wish not to have or not to be, what we like and what we don't like. Love and marriage and banquets and dances and springtime and wheat and fruit and wine are good. Hate and strife and downfall and death, disease, blight, and poison, are bad. A lamb is a good animal, a wolf or a tiger is a bad one, and frightening, especially in a pastoral society or tradition. "Any symbolism founded on food," says Frye, "is universal." [44] We can live in a city or a garden, not in a stony or weedy wilderness. If we rummage out all the ideas of the desirable and undesirable we can think of, they fall inevitably under the heads of the supernatural, the human, the animal, vegetable, and mineral, as Frye himself comes close to explaining in his allusion to the

[43] *Watt* (New York, 1959), p. 200.   [44] *Anatomy,* p. 118.

game of Twenty Questions. See the catalogues of apocalyptic and demonic imagery in the essay of 1951 and in the third essay of the *Anatomy*.[45] But the general problem of a literary theorist who would be a revolutionary leader with truisms is how to make them seem pregnant and novel. "One essential principle of archetypal criticism," Frye instructs us, "is that the individual and the universal forms of an image are identical, the reasons being too complicated for us just now." [46] Like Blake, Frye would number the streaks of the mythic tulip. But for the theorist there are some special difficulties. Not in the abstractionist and truistic half of the system, but in its needed complement the specific and the colorful, we come to the issue of the cliché. The cliché, as Rémy de Gourmont said in passages that have been well understood by the American New Critics, is more than a matter of triteness and repetition. In that sense, all of our established vocabulary is cliché. The true idea of the cliché (the offensive cliché) involves the notion of irrelevance, the impertinent gloss of a misplaced special effort to be bright. ("Do you live in New York? I like to visit New York. I wouldn't live in the place if you gave it to me.") Frye himself has given us a happy exposition of how this applies. In *The Well-Tempered Critic* [47] he speaks of a certain "mytho-historical" type of stock response, probably the "most

[45] And see the images of upper and lower, journeys of ascent and descent in the classical "topocosm" described in "New Directions from Old" (1960), *Fables of Identity*, pp. 58–65.

[46] "The Archetypes of Literature" (1951), *Fables of Identity*, p. 19. Cf. "Literature as Context: Milton's *Lycidas*" (1959), *Fables*, p. 120: "By archetype I mean a literary symbol, or cluster of symbols, which are used recurrently throughout literature, and thereby become conventional."

[47] *The Well-Tempered Critic*, pp. 125–26.

common" type. He had a student once who admired "Good King Wenceslas" because he thought it had been written in the thirteenth century. But this student lost all interest when Frye explained that it was in fact "a kind of Victorian singing commercial." This, adds Frye, was "only a very common form of misplaced concreteness." But the mythopoeic system of Frye himself is a wholesale indulgence in that very fallacy of misplaced concreteness. A cliché, being not simply a repetition, may even be ingenious and original (or at least novel). When a biographer of John Barrymore tells us that Barrymore took on "the Danish assignment" or that he decided to "draw on the black tights of the classic Scandinavian," we may never have heard these expressions before, but we feel their affinity for, if not identity with, the dismal kind of cliché. Similarly, to describe Hamlet's stage-tradition jump into Ophelia's grave as if it were an instance of the classic descent into the underworld is a cliché application of the archetype,[48] ingenious perhaps, but still a cliché, a mythopoeist's cliché. It is the same thing to call Leontes in *The Winter's Tale* a *senex iratus* out of the New Comedy,[49] or to describe Tom Sawyer and Becky Thatcher's adventures in the cave as a displaced version of the dragon-killing myth (thus raising in our minds irrelevant images of Theseus, St. George, and Beowulf), or to see Lemuel Gulliver, bound by the Lilliputians, as a parody Promethean figure,[50] or to see Belinda in *The Rape of the Lock* as a figure out of the Rape of Proserpine, or, even worse, to see Wordsworth's Lucy, "rolled round . . . with

---

[48] *Anatomy*, p. 140; "The Archetypes of Literature" (1951), *Fables of Identity*, p. 13.

[49] *A Natural Perspective*, p. 74.  [50] *Anatomy*, pp. 190, 321.

rocks, and stones, and trees," as an underground companion of the same unlucky goddess.[51] The type assumes the solidity of the character or action it is called in to "identify." The *tritos anthropos,* the third man used by Parmenides and Aristotle against the Platonic ideas, becomes in such a context once more a relevant invocation.[52] A universal idea ascends into the rainbow stratosphere of the archetypes and redescends to settle a cloak of exotic and unearned colors on the shoulders of some Shakespearean or Dickensian character. Warm gules indeed on Madeline's fair breast. Myth, like a dome of many-colored glass, stains the white radiance of anagogy. The Anima Mundi swarms with sputniks, Telstars, chattering back their advice for stability in the art market.

A lurid glow, a feeling of rituals enacted in the deepest recesses of the racial past, of a remotely primitive authentication, is no doubt generated by the appearance of Frye's Hallowe'en cast of characters and the mazes of their cyclic action. A "primitive response," we are told, is demanded of us.[53] "If we neutralize the archetype," says Meyer Abrams, "by eliminating dark allusions

---

[51] *Anatomy,* p. 183; "Literature as Context: Milton's *Lycidas"* (1959), *Fables of Identity,* p. 125. See also, e.g., Kingsley's Mary rowed in across the "cruel, crawling foam"—with a "faint coloring of the myth of Andromeda" (*Anatomy,* p. 36), Lord Jim as "a lineal descendant of the *miles gloriosus"* (*Anatomy,* p. 40), the detective-story murderer as a *pharmakos* pursued by a man-hunter (*Anatomy,* p. 46), and Rousseau's desire for a revolutionary revival of primitivism as "informed by the myth of the sleeping beauty" (*Anatomy,* p. 353).

[52] "The present facts," says Frye of the extreme historical versions of mythopoeia, "are being compared to their own shadows" (*Anatomy,* p. 108).

[53] *A Natural Perspective,* pp. 6, 64.

to 'primordial images' or 'the racial memory' or 'timeless depths,' archetypal criticism is drained of the mystique or pathos which is an important part of its present vogue." [54] And of course we can neutralize it. We must. The Ur-Myth, the Quest Myth, with all its complications, its cycles, acts, scenes, characters, and special symbols, is not a historical fact. And this is so not only in the obvious sense that the stories are not true, but in another sense, which I think we tend to forget and which mythopoeic writing does much to obscure: that such a coherent, cyclic, and encyclopedic system, such a monomyth, cannot be shown ever to have evolved actually, either from or with ritual, anywhere in the world, or ever anywhere to have been entertained in whole or even in any considerable part. We are talking about the myth of myth. As Frye himself, in his moments of cautionary vision, observes, the "derivation" of the literary genres from the quest myth is "logical," not historical.[55] That is, it is made up according to desire, by the imagination of the critic. That brave old world, that had such people in it, is a conglomerate of extrapolations out of actual Greek literature by Frazer and other Cambridge anthropologists, of reports and speculations about modern primitive or isolated peoples, and of assumptions taken, whether explicitly or implicitly, from the psychology of the collective unconscious.

[54] "The Correspondent Breeze" (1957), in *English Romantic Poets,* ed. Meyer Abrams, p. 49.

[55] *Anatomy,* p. 108; "The Archetypes of Literature" (1951), *Fables of Identity,* p. 17: "It is only when we try to expound the derivation chronologically that we find ourselves writing pseudo-historical fictions. . . ." Pages 16–17 stress Frazer and Jung's *Psychology of the Unconscious* (1912). Cf. "New Directions from Old" (1960), *Fables,* p. 66, and "Literature as Context: Milton's *Lycidas*" (1959), *Fables,* p. 119.

"Anthropology tells us," says Frye in 1947. "Psychology tells us." [56] It is true that Frye, after an early appeal to both Frazer and Jung, has vigorously disclaimed any reliance on them or on any "chronological" derivation of myth at all.[57] He may well disclaim Frazer and Jung. They may be an embarrassment; they are not strictly needed. What *is* needed, however, is some constant implication or intimation of the primordial, the more mysterious the better. And such an implication is surely present. For "primitive" and other terms, nearly synonymous, in Frye's system, let him subsitute throughout simply "universal"; for "myth," substitute "story" or "idea" or even "preternatural" story or idea; for "archetype," simply "type" or "model." And let him remove the Greek and Latin names of his archetypal figures, especially the proper names, and his broad appeals to both the Bible and Greek mythology.[58] The loss of blood, the destruction of the system, will be terrible to contemplate. Let him remove, for that matter, simply the historic cycle from myth to irony, the "Great Year," in the first essay of the *Anatomy*. And let him not, as he has recently done, bring out Livy and Donatus—or any of the several other rumors of late antiquity which are known to classical scholarship [59]—as if these could improve the insufficient argu-

[56] *Fearful Symmetry* (Princeton, 1947), p. 424.

[57] *Anatomy*, pp. 108–12.     [58] *The Educated Imagination*, pp. 46–47.

[59] Frye, *A Natural Perspective*, pp. 54, 58, invokes Livy vii.2.6–7 and Donatus, the latter [in fact Euanthius] as reported by Thomas Lodge. Only the first sentence of the passage quoted from Lodge is in fact from Donatus-Euanthius. See Donatus, ⟨*Euanthius de Fabula*⟩, i.1–4: "Initium tragoediae et commediae a rebus divinis est incohatum, quibus pro fructibus vota solventes operabantur antiqui. . . . res tragicae longe ante comicas inventae." For other authorities of late antiquity, see A. W. Pickard-Cambridge, *Dithyramb, Comedy and Tragedy* (Oxford, 1927), pp. 97–107.

ment which has all along rested on the brief and obscure passages of extrapolated history in Aristotle's *Poetics*.

If we take Frye at his word and attempt to deduce his system "logically," we will reject it, for the structure which he shows us is, as I have been saying, divided between truism and *ad libitum* fantasy. What really happens is that we yield to these apparitions a kind of suspended judgment, because we fear, or hope, that behind them some kind of historical or quasi-historical validation is only waiting for the right moment to be wheeled into the arena. They extort the same kind of respect as men from Mars on radio programs in days long before Mariner IV had sent back photographs revealing the great improbability of higher life on that "sterile promontory."

A certain fictive coloring manifests itself throughout the mythopoeic exposition in a number of other ways. For instance, in a frequently original employment of terminology. Frye needs not only his own cast of characters and his special plots but his own language or vocabulary of displaced diction—derangement of epitaphs. It is a strange language. Consider, for instance, in the Polemical Introduction of 1957, the term "tropical," with its marginal or archaic meaning of "figurative," apparently introduced here mainly because of its oddity.[60] It gives the reader something to wonder about and thus may make him fail to realize the momentary bizarre focus by which study of figures can be equated with "the rhetoric of verbal ornament" and at the same time can be imputed to social and moral prejudice. Frye's vocabulary is not an accident but a necessary engine for the

[60] *Anatomy*, p. 21. Perhaps Kenneth Burke is partly to blame, and no doubt Hamlet.

projection of some of his slanted visions. Despite frequent complaints about merely "rhetorical" kinds of literary criticism, Frye will also assert, in other contexts, that rhetoric necessarily intervenes between grammar and logic and hence that there can be no really logical argument in words.[61] This is in effect his defense of his own style, which we have already seen in different phrasing. Consider, for a second example, the term "literal," at the bottom level of symbol-reading in the second essay of the *Anatomy,* whereas "literal" in the well-known medieval system, as Frye himself labors to point out,[62] means something which corresponds to the second level in his essay, the realistic "descriptive." Frye divides the term "literal," in his own way, between a tautology—"a poem cannot be literally anything but a poem"— and the notion of some kind of sheer verbal (or "letter") music and sheer verbal (or "letter") imagery, apparently independent of any sign value the words may have.[63] Nobody else would use "literal" as Frye uses it here. The very thin slice of symbolism which he is talking about ought to be called, if anything, the "alphabetical" or perhaps the "phonemic," but such a name would advertise the fact that no such kind of criticism ever really occurs. To take a simpler and more sweeping example, let us not forget the term "displacement," a key term in Frye's system, itself a strange displacement,[64] by which reality becomes anoma-

[61] *Anatomy,* pp. 335–37, 350.          [62] *Anatomy,* pp. 76, 116.

[63] *Anatomy,* pp. 77–78.

[64] *Anatomy,* pp. 136–37. The innocent-looking term "genre" is another curiosity, functioning in the second essay to refer only to the "mythical" or "archetypal" phase of reading, but turning up at the head of the fourth essay ("Theory of Genres") to describe a rhythmic layout of literature according to transactions between author and audience (epic, dramatic, prose fictional, lyric).

lous, and "pure un-inhibited" fantasy the norm. And notice the curiously willful use of the term "imagination" and several related terms in the essay of 1961 "Myth, Fiction, and Displacement," by which he manages to put Coleridge "in the tradition of critical naturalism,"[65] because forsooth Coleridge conceived a "secondary imagination" and thus avoided the frenzy of the total identifying "vision."[66]

Frye says in the first essay of the *Anatomy* (on the status of protagonists) that his alignments of "high" and "low" are not evaluative but only "diagrammatic."[67] This, as I may already have suggested, must be questioned. Evaluations, and diagrammatic evaluations, do obtrude all through these essays. Consider, for instance, the verbal critics, the New Critics, groveling in the wintry cellar of verbal irony,[68] and at the other end of things the

[65] *Fables of Identity,* pp. 29–30.

[66] "Towards Defining an Age of Sensibility" (1956), *Fables of Identity,* pp. 134, 136. Or notice how myths are carefully, even insistently, differentiated from folk tales (the latter lacking the element of divinity) in Frye's essay of 1961 "Myth, Fiction, and Displacement" (*Fables,* pp. 31–32), but in his Shakespeare lectures of 1963, *Cymbeline* is a "pure folk tale," which three pages later adds to Shakespeare's problem comedies a "primitive mythical dimension" (*A Natural Perspective,* pp. 67, 70).

[67] *Anatomy,* p. 34. Cf. pp. 335, 350; and "How True a Twain" (1962), *Fables of Identity,* p. 93, on "high" and "low" themes in Shakespeare's Sonnets. In an early essay on Yeats, Frye quotes a warning from Blake against "mathematic form" or the "Euclidean paraphernalia of diagrams, figures, tables of symbols and the like, which inevitably appear when symbolism is treated as a dead language." The examples of Elizabethan handbooks and commentaries and that of Yeats's commentary on Blake which Frye adduces in the same essay do not seem to have warned him that he himself was in any danger ("Yeats and the Language of Symbolism" [1947], *Fables,* pp. 218–19, 231–32).

[68] *Anatomy,* pp. 65–66.

heroes on the high sunlit plains of myth and romance lifting their gaze to the apocalytic windows of the morning. But, to put value aside, diagrammatic descriptions ought at least to be capable of diagram. If they are not, there would seem to be a grave question as to what they are saying. Frye is really, in the long run, not very careful with his diagramming. In the very complicated third essay of the *Anatomy,* on the mythic cycle, spring is comedy, and summer is romance. And much turns on that analogy. But in the essay on "The Archetypes" of 1951,[69] spring had been romance, and summer had been comedy. And in the collected *Fables* of 1963 Frye does not scruple to reproduce that essay without adjustment and without warning to his audience. Presumably we are not expected to notice such misalignments or to boggle at them. The fact is that Frye moves from the descending *sequence* of his first essay—romance, high mimesis (most tragedy, central tragedy), low mimesis (most comedy), irony—to the embarrassment of a very different *sequence* of "broader categories" in the third essay: spring (comedy), summer (romance), autumn (tragedy), winter (irony-satire).[70] This no doubt has something to do with the complexities that emerge in the asserted correspondence of the first and second three of the six phases of each season with its adjacent seasons.[71] The key pages are 177: second three of comedy (spring) with the second three of romance (summer); 219: first three of romance with the first three of tragedy (autumn); 236: second three of tragedy with the second three of

[69] *Kenyon Review,* XIII (Winter, 1951), 103–5.

[70] *Anatomy,* pp. 34, 37, 154, 157, 163, 206. Cf. p. 75, "the sense of reality . . . far higher in tragedy than in comedy." The "parallel" between the five descending modes of the first essay and the ascending phases of symbolism in the second is explicitly asserted (p. 116).

[71] "The four seasons of the year being the type" (*Anatomy,* p. 160).

satire (winter); 225: first three of satire with the first three of comedy. "There are thus four main types of mythical movement: within romance, within experience, down, and up." [72] "With Centric and Eccentric scribbl'd o'er, Cycle and Epicycle, Orb in Orb." Superimposed fourth-of-July pinwheels, with a reversing sequence of rocket engines, may give a dim idea of the pyrotechnics involved here. By a proper attention to the *terminally* climactic structure of the spring and autumn seasons and the *medially* climactic structure of the winter and summer seasons, Frye might have worked out his diagram and might have succeeded in whirling his twenty-four literary subcategories at least *consistently* around the seasonal cycle. But even that would not have paralleled the pattern of his first essay, and furthermore it would not have helped the supposedly primordial and archetypal notion of the Spenglerian [73] four-season cycle. For the truth is that man's consciousness of seasonal change has varied much in various ages and climates. The ancient Greeks, as Sigmund Freud reminds us, generally distinguished only three seasons (spring, summer, and winter), the three Horai or daughters of Zeus and Themis.[74] The variations of lunar, solar, and pluvial calendars in Buddhist, Hindu, and Muslim cultures (three, six, and two being apparently favorite numbers) are too complicated for the present moment.[75] *Winter* and *summer* are the continuous, ancient, and

[72] *Anatomy,* p. 162. Romance and satire are complete cycles within the larger cycle of tragedy and comedy (pp. 198, 239).

[73] "Yeats and the Language of Symbolism" (1947), *Fables of Identity,* p. 224; "Quest and Cycle in *Finnegans Wake*" (1957), *Fables,* p. 258.

[74] "The Theme of the Three Caskets," *Collected Papers* (New York, 1959), IV, 244–56.

[75] "Festivals and Fasts," in James Hastings, ed., *Encyclopedia of Religion and Ethics* (Edinburgh, 1937), V, 837, 868; Rhadagovinda Basak, "The

Germanic names of seasons in English, and these two seasons prevail in Old English heroic poetry. The astronomical and Roman sophistication of the four-seasonal system finds its way only later into the English popular and poetic consciousness.[76]

The four seasons, as they function in Frye's system, are just about as primitive as the four strokes of a piston in a Rolls Royce engine. Except that Frye's Rolls Royce will not actually roll.

I find it difficult at this point not to be reminded of genealogy. Frye, as we know from his *Fearful Symmetry,* 1947, and from a recent lecture, "The Road of Excess," found the interpretation of Blake the beginning of a revolution in his own reading of all poetry.[77] He gives perhaps a further, if less deliberate, clue in his essay of 1956 "Towards Defining an Age of Sensibility," where he achieves a definition which embraces Blake himself in the same madly visionary perspective with Ossian and Rowley.[78] "I Believe," wrote Blake, in a rebuke to the naturalism of Wordsworth's *Essay* of 1815, "I Believe both Macpherson & Chatterton,

---

Hindu Conception of the Natural World," in Kenneth W. Morgan, ed., *The Religion of the Hindus* (New York, 1953), p. 96; Maurice Gaudefroy-Demombynes, *Muslim Institutions,* tr. by John P. MacGregor (London, 1954), p. 182.

[76] Nils Erik Enkvist, *The Seasons of the Year: Chapters on a Motif from Beowulf to the Shepherd's Calendar* (Helsingfors, 1957), pp. 1–5, 196–210.

[77] *Fearful Symmetry,* pp. 10–11, 418, 424; "The Road of Excess," in Bernice Slote, ed., *Myth and Symbol* (Lincoln, 1963), pp. 3–20.

[78] ". . . where the metaphor is conceived as part of an oracular and half-ecstatic process, there is a direct identification in which the poet himself is involved. . . . it is in this psychological self-identification that the central 'primitive' quality of this age really emerges" (*Fables of Identity,* p. 136).

that what they say is Ancient Is so." "Precious memorandums," growled Wordsworth, "from the pocketbook of the blind Ossian." Only "the boy, Chatterton," already a forger, had ventured to imitate them. Wordsworth's taste and judgment were accurate. Still he was not far enough removed to have much perspective on the phase of primitivism he was examining. Macpherson's plush-covered Gaelic Homer was Macpherson's own literary idiom and, such as it was, a genuine literary creation. At the moment of its publication, however, it needed the excuse of a feigned antiquity. Chatterton too invented a scenery and a cast of characters—Rowley, Cannynge, John a Iscam, Aella, Sir Simon de Burton, and all the rest—and above all he created a language—as truly a poetic idiom, an expressive forgery out of the morphemic and phonemic elements of his native English—as Spenser's archaic "no language" had been or as Burns's partly synthetic Ayrshire Scots would soon be. Yet for Chatterton it was equally important for getting his idiom launched that he claim the warrant of an antique authenticity. With Macpherson and Chatterton we have a kind of expressiveness balanced so nicely with a sham antiquity that it is difficult to say which gives more support to the other.[79] Blake as a boy tried out both idioms briefly, before

[79] "The Ossian and Rowley poems," says Frye correctly, "are not simple hoaxes: they are pseudepigrapha . . . they take what is psychologically primitive, the oracular process of composition, and project it as something historically primitive" ("Towards Defining an Age of Sensibility" [1956], *Fables of Identity,* p. 136). See the savage, the lunatic, the lover, and the poet treated repeatedly in *Fables*—e.g., "Towards Defining an Age of Sensibility" (1956), p. 136; "Blake after Two Centuries" (1957), p. 141; "Literature as Context: Milton's *Lycidas*" (1959), p. 128; "The Imaginative and the Imaginary" (1962), pp. 152, 154. The "fraudulent miracles," the

entering as a man upon his own construction of myth, in purest English, line, and color, though in wildest apocalyptic fantasy. Blake solved the problem of belief in credentials by a simple fusion. No doubt there was little difference between the sense in which he said, "I Believe both Macpherson & Chatterton," and the sense in which he believed in his own Urizen, Orc, Los, and all the rest of his varicose *dramatis personae.*

The eighteenth-century age of sensibility and much of the nineteenth century tended to validate literature by an appeal to the authentic heart and mind of the primitive folk and of the closely related childish and naïve. We recognize today, at least when we are wide awake and thinking about any identifiable time or place, that that heart and mind are no more authentic than any other. So far as that simple and sincere mind exists—outside of modern myths—it can be mistaken, uncouth, outlandish, stupid, and brutal, at least as much as any other. Yet such loyalties die hard. It is possible that we in our own way (we scholars, especially, saturated in our devotion to the past) have been turning to another deep part of the eighteenth-century preromantic mind—the inclination to authenticate certain visions by the method of forgery. Poetry itself is nowadays conceived, at least by some of our most progressive thinkers, as a kind of forgery, that is, a bold visionary mistake. "Literature, like mythology," writes our chief authority and the subject of this paper, "is largely an art of misleading analogies and mistaken identities." [80] Extend this idea to criticism,

---

"charlatanism" of Madame Blavatsky, says Frye, are "less a reflection on her than on an age that compelled her to express herself in such devious ways" ("Yeats and the Language of Symbolism" [1947], *Fables,* p. 221).

[80] "Myth, Fiction, and Displacement" (1961), *Fables of Identity,* p. 35.

as seventy-five years ago Oscar Wilde showed the way. The idea of poetry as myth will readily extrapolate to the idea of criticism as myth, and thus, by the shortest of leaps, to that of criticism as forgery. Facts, apparently, are not needed. The deduction of our whole argument is logical, not historical. Still the envisioned facts of a literary ur-history and a prehistory serve the very useful purpose of suggesting a kind of antique authority and terminus for veneration. A "primitive response" is "demanded." It is no doubt as futile to try to bring mythopoeic criticism to the measure of observation and reason as it was for W. W. Skeat to normalize the language of Chatterton's Rowley—by which he succeeded only in purging Chatterton of his main poetic value. Visionary criticism enjoys, I think, not quite the immunities of visionary poetry. Yet this kind of criticism may be in a sense, in its own moment and for its own creator, indefeasible. For the rest of us, what if the cast of critical characters should all turn out to be phantoms? The priest of the Sacred Grove at Nemi "too," wrote Frazer near the end of his great work, he "too, for all the quaint garb he wears and the gravity with which he stalks across the stage, is merely a puppet, and it is time to unmask him before laying him up in the box." [81] "These our actors, As I foretold you, were all spirits and Are melted into thin air, into thin air."

[81] *The Golden Bough,* 3d ed., X (1913), vi. Cf. Stanley Edgar Hyman, *The Tangled Bank* (New York, 1962), p. 266.

# GEOFFREY H. HARTMAN

*

## Ghostlier Demarcations

"The dark Religions are departed and sweet Science reigns."

Blake

COMMENTING on Aristotle's *Poetics,* the first systematic criticism known to us, S. H. Butcher remarks that its author is preeminently "a Greek summing up Greek experience." Northrop Frye, the latest and most ambitious exponent of a systematic criticism, can hardly be described as a Canadian summing up Canadian experience, or even as a scholar summing up the experience of English literature. His situation is so different from Aristotle's that to express it it is tempting to use Copernicus' image of the "virile man standing in the sun . . . overlooking the planets." I do not intend this image to suggest a premature deification, but to describe a new vantage point with its promise of mastery and also its enormously expanded burden of sight. Certainly no literary thinker, systematic or not, has attained so global a point of view of literature. The nearest parallels to this achievement come from other though related disciplines: there is Mircea Eliade's work in comparative mythology, or André Malraux's in the history of art.

It is the question of point of view, or of the critic's situation, I shall be initially concerned with. For although Frye has said that his system exists for the insights and not the other way around, the excitement, the liberation, the play, as well as the most serious claim he makes is the possibility of system. Frye is an overreacher, a man with hubris, but it is a methodical hubris, a heuristic and applied attitude. There is, in other words, a more-than-intellectual aspect to system-making on such a scale. Literary criticism remains an expressive act; and despite its claims to objectivity, its moral and intellectual ends mingle. If Aristotle is a Greek summing up the experience of his culture, we should be able to discern the *polis* of Northrop Frye, and what visionary politics are his.

## I THE SITUATION OF THE CRITIC

Literature has not always been the property or interest of the many. Some, even today, think that the *paidea* of the New Criticism, the attempt to open literature to the direct understanding of students of any background, is undesirable or doomed to failure. It may not please those who know the great differences in pedagogical method between the New Critics and Northrop Frye to have me begin by suggesting that Frye is part of a single modern movement to democratize criticism and demystify the muse. I would go further and say that Frye is our most radical demystifier of criticism even though his great achievement is the recovery of the demon, or of the intrinsic role of Romance in the human imagination. His importance to literary history proper is as a topographer of the Romance imagination in its direct and displaced forms. But his service to the ongoing need to have greater numbers of persons participate in the imaginative life, to open the covenant of education until the difference between persons is really "ghostly," only a matter of intenser or lesser participation, in this he continues the vision of those first struck in the nineteenth century with the possibility of universal education, and who felt with Victor Hugo that the multiplication of books was comparable to the multiplying of loaves of bread.

Demystification begins in Frye with the very concept of system. This concept should be distinguished, at first, from the particular system furthered. To systematize criticism is to universalize it, to put its intellectual or spiritual techniques into the hands of every intelligent person, of every child even. To imagine children of the future performing little Anatomies as easily as they now do basic operations in mathematics may not be everyone's Utopia, but we should recall that Frye is ambitious only with respect to the possibility of system and not to his particular version of it. Yet it must be pointed out that he fuses, or confuses, two notions of universality. One is the scientific, and holds that the criticism of literature should be pursued as a coherent and systematic study, which, like mathematics, has elementary principles explainable to anyone. The other is evangelical, and holds that critics have stood like priests between literature and those desiring to participate in it, whereas even a child should be able to be instructed in the principles that make art nourishing. When Frye says "the only guarantee that a subject is theoretically coherent is its ability to have its elementary principles taught to children," [1] it is hard to tell the scientific from the evangelical notion. Frye's scientism is therefore the opposite of exclusionary: he does not seek to over-dignify criticism or scholarship but to place its basic principles and their creative development in the hands of every earnest reader. "What critics now have is a mystery-religion without a gospel . . . they are initiates who can communicate, or quarrel, only with one another." [2]

But who put the mystery Frye wants to purge into criticism? Nobody: Frye is indicating that unorganized innocence falls prey to the latest compulsions in taste—to casual, sentimental, or social value-judgments. This is the more likely as the assumption of innocence, in literary scholarship, takes the form of an appeal to pragmatism, commonsense, or impartiality. The unsystematic critic considers his lack of system proof that he cannot possibly be prejudiced. Frye, I think, would hesitate to go further and to accuse specific groups of surrounding the study of literature with a mystique. Yet the feature of his system that has caused most protest is precisely his relegation of certain kinds of value-judg-ment to the history of taste and his resolute exclusion of them from criticism. If there is a mystique, it lies here, in the conviction challenged by him that literature is to be used as a training ground for the élite judgment.

Such a conviction is a carry-over from the time when Classics were at the center of humanistic studies, and English did not exist as an academic field. The Classics were studied not for them-

---

[1] "The Developing Imagination," in *Learning in Language and Litera-ture* (Cambridge, Mass., 1963), p. 33. Cf. *Anatomy of Criticism* (Princeton, 1957), p. 14.
[2] *Anatomy*, p. 14.

selves but as part of the proper education for the upper classes, composed of administrators, churchmen, and statesmen. When English, a mere baby among academic disciplines, won its freedom in the 1920s and 1930s (Tillyard's *The Muse Unchained* records vividly part of that emancipation), it engendered its own protective and self-dignifying mystique. It did this by assuming the mantle of Classical studies and claiming for English literature the same function of training the judgment. It also insisted that this training was best provided by the immediacies of vernacular literature. We may admire the careful scrutiny, the chaste inquisition brought to bear on the vernacular status of words, or on the consciousness organizing them, which now for the first time enters literary studies, and still acknowledge that the object of the new discipline was not a total or synoptic conception of literature but the training, through literature, of a specific and judicious sensibility. And it is hard not to feel the breath of a mystique in the following recommendation of the "English School," which shows how thoroughly Leavis, who wrote it, adapted and refined the Classicist emphasis on the importance of judgment:

The essential discipline of an English School is the literary-critical; it is a true discipline, only in an English School if anywhere will it be fostered, and it is irreplaceable. It trains, in a way no other discipline can, intelligence and sensibility together, cultivating a sensitiveness and precision of response and a delicate integrity of intelligence— intelligence that integrates as well as analyses and must have pertinacity and staying power as well as delicacy.[3]

[3] Quoted by Fred Inglis, "Professor Northrop Frye and the Study of Literature," *Centennial Review*, IX (1965), 325–26. On the importance of the "Vernacular Matrix" for modern criticism, see W. J. Ong, s.j., *The Barbarian Within* (New York, 1962), ch. x.

Whether or not Frye's expulsion of rationalized "taste" from the history of criticism is viable, its purpose is to cleanse that discipline of a sporadically chauvinistic cult of culture. His "categorial criticism" is a direct challenge to the English mystique of English Studies. It bypasses personalistic judgment and the tutorial approach to literature. Instead of the tutor there is the system, instead of judgments reposing on a precarious blend of moral, verbal, literary sensibility, there is the extroversion of archetypes and the free yet controlled establishment of a criticism without walls. The act of appreciating literature has its private pleasures, but it becomes criticism by becoming extramural—by interpretations that link the Classics to English literature and all literature to a total form that reveals archetypal features. Frye's concern is with a point of view determined by culture as such, rather than by a particular culture, tradition, or line.

This raises the question of what Frye means by total form, and obliges us to turn from his concept of system to the system itself. The intellectual problems here are very great, but ours are greater: for Frye is an eloquent man who somewhere has provided an answer to every question. What must therefore be judged is not his comprehensiveness, which is extraordinary, or his intentions, which are the best since Matthew Arnold, but how well he has dealt with problems every literary critic faces whatever his attitude toward systematic thought. These problems must center, at some point, on how the individual literary work is related to art's general function in consciousness or society. "No discussion of beauty," says Frye, "can confine itself to the formal relations of the isolated work of art; it must consider, too, the participation of the work of art in the vision of the goal of social effort, the idea of complete and classless civilization." [4]

If we were to apply the technique of "extracting the myth" to Frye himself, we would come on a pastoral motif: "The hungry sheep look up, and are not fed." His critical system moves in the same direction as the history of art it seeks to liberate—away from the closed culture, the closed society, the priest-interpreter, the critic's critic. Properly understood he appears as a knight in a continuing quest: that of removing the dragon from the hoard, or mystery from communion.

## II THE CONCEPT OF TOTAL FORM

In saying that Frye aims at a "criticism without walls," I was implicitly adapting a phrase used by André Malraux. He remarked that modern techniques of reproduction had created in the visual arts a "museum without walls," and made the world's masterpieces available to every viewer. But he also noted that this had changed profoundly our conception of the uniqueness of the artifact which is now universally distributed and no longer in a special relation to its place of origin. The more transportable the sacred objects of a culture, the more abstract our notion of art tends to be. "You do not put gods in a museum," says Malraux, "the gods there become paintings." Modern photography converts all "historical" artifacts into "free" works of art. It robs them of their original context and reveals through synopsis and juxtaposition a more coherent or self-referring entity.

Frye, whose concern is chiefly with the verbal arts, where the revolution of which Malraux is talking began with Gutenberg,

[4] *Anatomy,* p. 348.

does not stress the technological factor. "The revolution," he writes, "is not simply in technology but in spiritual productive power."[5] Yet we have seen that his very concept of system combines a technological result with an evangelical purpose. If the Bible had not been unchained by Gutenberg and the Reformers, and if this liberation had not continued until the gods sit as books in our libraries, the kind of analysis Frye calls "archetypal" might not have come about.

For there is no mystery about "archetype." The archetype is simply the typical at the highest power of literary generalization. The typical was valued in the eighteenth century for its universality within the context of polite society; and the archetypal emerges when the concept of a literary universe, made possible by technology, is substituted for that of polite society. And just as the world of the typical is society perfected, with its hieratic structure, its vertical line of authority; so the world of the archetypal is not some primitive communion but Arnold's and Malraux's "complete and classless civilization" with its intersubjective structure and its authority derived purely from a continuing vision transmitted by the arts.

Thus art contributes to a supreme fiction, an archetypal or total form, which is the forerunner of a new, demystified theory of participation. The Marxist concept of types, the Western historians' concept of topoi, the renewal of interest in biblical typology, the attempt to see art as an especially concrete sort of universal—as well as the varieties of myth-criticism—show how deeply modern literary theory is implicated in transcending the view that art is a private or élitist enterprise.

[5] *Anatomy,* p. 344.

Historically the new theory of participation was given its most radical statement by the Romantics. "Would to God that all the Lord's people were prophets," writes Blake, quoting the reply of Moses to those who wished him to restrict the divine vision.[6] Art must be freed from mystery, from the very thing Mallarmé cultivated as "le mystère dans les lettres." It is to be within the reach of all and practically a biological inheritance: "The mystery in the greatness of *King Lear* or *Macbeth* comes not from concealment but from revelation, not from something unknown or unknowable in the work, but from something unlimited in it."[7]

The emphasis on demystification also helps with the curious flatness of archetypes as Frye conceives them. Archetypes are not hidden but almost too open—if we do not easily spot them it is because we expect the wrong kind of mystery. Frye does not practice depth-criticism or depth-psychology; in this he differs absolutely from Jung, and it is impossible to attach an occult or, simply, ontological virtue to the structures he derives from mythology. This flattening out of the mythic substance is like transforming a landscape into a map, but also like opening a closed book. Archetypal analysis brings art into the public domain and makes it what nature was to Sir Thomas Browne, a "manuscript expans'd unto the eyes of all."

When we recall the rejection of myths of depth in contemporary literature and phenomenology, and when we think of how Wallace Stevens tries to return to a fundamental insight of the Romantics obscured even in him by traces of Symbolist cultism, we easily perceive Frye's link to the modern movement which insists on demystification. The "virile man standing in the

---

[6] Epigraph to *Milton;* Numbers XI:29.    [7] *Anatomy,* p. 88.

sun" begins to merge with Stevens' virile poet and central man who declares he has outlived the esoteric muses: "No longer do I believe that there is a mystic muse, sister of the Minotaur. This is another of the monsters I had for nurse, whom I have wasted. I am myself a part of what is real, and it is my own speech and the strength of it, this only, that I hear or ever shall." [8]

Yet archetypes, unmysterious as they are, cast a shadow. It has often been remarked that the particularity of the literary work may be obscured by too great or synoptic an angle of vision. Archetypal analysis can degenerate into an abstract thematics where the living pressure of mediations is lost and all connections are skeletonized. These faults appear clearly in the little book on T. S. Eliot and the essay on Milton's "Lycidas," inexpensive world tours of myth. Yet what we are facing here is not merely the weaker side of a method but something inherent in any response to a dilemma posed by the very promise of technology. "What we have to defend today," Marshall McLuhan has said, "is not the values developed in any particular culture or by any one mode of communication. Modern technology presumes to attempt a total transformation of man and his environment. This calls in turn for an inspection and defense of all human values." [9] The need for a global perspective is evident.

Every greater critic has recognized this situation, which demands the rejection or else redemption of technology, but in any case a total rather than piecemeal approach. Yet few have accepted

[8] "The Figure of the Youth as Virile Poet," *The Necessary Angel* (New York, 1951).

[9] "Sight, Sound and the Fury," *The Commonweal,* LX (April 9, 1954), 11.

the challenge so optimistically as Northrop Frye. Ortega y Gasset writes of the dehumanization, and not humanization, of modern art; and Walter Benjamin, in "The Work of Art in the Era of Its Technical Reproduction," sees more sharply than anyone the estranging influence of technology on culture. Technology, he asserts, will transform works of art into exhibition pieces and consumer goods, and so destroy what he calls their *aura*.[10] And Erich Auerbach toward the end of *Mimesis,* a book almost the obverse in temperament to Frye's *Anatomy,* foresees the withering away of those fully individuated civilizations of which he has just written as if already their last historian. What, then, is the future of historical criticism? Can the aura of the individual work be saved? Or is Frye's totalizing approach, which looks more and more Olympian, the true alternative? The theory of literature, like literature itself, seems to have entered the crisis stage in its attempt to find the relation of the particular, the "dreadful sundry of this world," to any authentic concept of totality.

## III  THE COURSE OF THE PARTICULAR

The possibilities of myth as a structural principle were brought to light by the practice of certain writers in the Symbolist era. Yeats and Joyce, T. S. Eliot said in a famous essay of 1923, substituted "the mythical method" for the "narrative method." Eliot had resolved the problem of the "dreadful sundry" by similar means. The new method, according to him, "is simply a way of controlling, of ordering, of giving shape and significance to the

---

[10] "Das Kunstwerk im Zeitalter seiner technischen Reproduzierbarkeit," *Schriften* (Frankfurt a.M., 1955), I, 366–405.

immense panorama of futility and anarchy which is contemporary history."[11] It is clear that the substitution of mythical for narrative method, in literature or criticism, expresses the difficulty of finding ideas of order within secular history.

Frye, however, does not emphasize the heuristic character of the new method. Although his system is frankly speculative, it rarely allows for counterpoint or opposition between the historical and the mythical. Supremely eclectic, Frye melts what many would consider as contraries into one system of alternative yet concordant approaches. What counterpoint exists is for the richness of the melody: he does not make us feel the problematic situation of either writer or critic, or any sign of that divided consciousness which the mythical method affirms by remaining an artifice in Yeats and Joyce.[12]

To bring out the discords between Frye's mode of criticism and a more historical one, let us consider a model of the act of interpretation furnished by biblical hermeneutics. When Donne, in

[11] "Ulysses, Order, and Myth." First published in *The Dial.* Eliot's practice may also be indebted to the rediscovery of the ritual origin of literary forms by the Cambridge anthropologists. See his somewhat condescending remarks on Jane Harrison and others in "Euripides and Professor Murray" (1920).

[12] Though Mr. Fletcher has begun to study Frye as what Kierkegaard would have called a "subjective thinker," Frye's strength lies in that "grammar" of imagery, or "morphology" of myth, derived from Blake and Yeats, which has allowed literary criticism to be—for the first time— truly systematic (synchronic) rather than historical (diachronic). He is better, in other words, at respecting the identity of mythical and systemic (an identity glimpsed by Vico and elaborated by French anthropologists from Durkheim to Lévi-Strauss) than the difference between mythical-systemic and historical. He is closest to Plato, for whom, as he observes in the *Anatomy,* "the ultimate acts of apprehension were either mathematical or mythical."

his Sermons, uses the expression "the intention of the Holy Ghost *in that place*," the word "place" refers to one or more of three things: topos, or figure of speech; context; locality. These relations of word to "place" also situate secular literature in its particularity. Thus the question of verbal or internal context can be equated with that of the temporal medium of the literary work; the question of topoi or figures with that of the authenticity of myth or figures derived from myth; and the question of the relation of words to native place with the aim of conventional histories to understand the literary work *in situ* by recovering its lexical and social ambiance.

What does Frye have to say on these matters which are essential to any historically based criticism? His attitude toward the fact that literature unfolds in time rather than quasi-simultaneously in space is puzzling. It would be possible to apply his type of analysis to the visual arts as well as to the verbal, for he stands back from poem or play as from a picture. A full-fledged example of the pictorial stance is his book on the development of Shakespearean comedy (*A Natural Perspective*), where he identifies structural similarities by removing himself to a "middle distance." In fact, as is well known, Frye's concept of literary structure is consciously spatial. It depends on a disjunction between our immediate experience of literature, which is guided by the tempo of the work, and criticism, which lays out the completed pattern spatially. "When a critic," he writes, "deals with a work of literature, the most natural thing for him to do is to freeze it, to ignore its movement in time and look at it as a completed pattern of words with all its parts existing simultaneously." [13] In the *Anat-*

[13] "Myth, Fiction, and Displacement" (1961), *Fables of Identity: Studies in Poetic Mythology* (New York, 1963), p. 21.

*omy,* this disjunction is presented as fundamental to the establishment of criticism as a progressive body of knowledge.

Unfortunately it is also an evasion of the whole problem of
temporality. With the related question of the unity of the literary
work, this problem has been the single most important topic of
poetics. It is true that systematic thought on temporality, starting
with Lessing and renewed by Heidegger, is mainly German. Yet
Helen Gardner expresses the identical concern when she says
that "the discovery of a work's center, the source of its life in all
its parts, and response to its total movement—a word I prefer
to 'structure,' for time is inseparable from our apprehension of
works of literature—is to me the purpose of critical activity." [14]
One of the most formal differences of literature is omitted if we
cannot encompass by reflection its moving power in time.

Frye's practice here is preferable to his theory. In his concern
not to isolate the work of art, but to let it flow into a larger realm
of discourse, he often perfects the example of G. Wilson Knight,
who first applied a "spatial" analysis to Shakespeare in the *Wheel
of Fire* (1930).[15] Frye on Beckett, Shakespeare, or Wallace

[14] *The Business of Criticism* (Oxford, 1959), pp. 23–24. One wonders
why Frye has not made greater use of Mircea Eliade's argument that
literary time remains basically mythical, because literature submerges us
in a "strange" time, and it is the character of myth to cure or at least
purify temporality by a ritual "going back" to the origins (anamnesis).
The spatializing habit of all structuralist analysis of the imagination has
been ably defended by a French work devoted to "archetypology." See
Gilbert Durand, *Les Structures Anthropologiques de l'Imaginaire* (1st ed.,
Paris, 1960).

[15] "One must be prepared to see the whole play in space as well as in
time. It is natural in analysis to pursue the steps of the tale in sequence,
noticing the logic that connects them, regarding those essentials that Aris-

Stevens can even be compared with the structuralist critics in Europe and America, with writers like Bachelard, Poulet, Lucien Goldmann, René Girard, J. Hillis Miller, and (*sui generis*) Leslie Fiedler. Also in search of the "total form," they insist that the bounding lines of the individual work are to be subordinated to larger patterns revealed by decomposing those outlines. But for them this form cannot finally be expressed in literary or mythical terms: it merges with an analysis of society, consciousness, and language. Although Frye posits the goal of society, and art's drive toward it, he does not specify what has separated man from his vision or into what temporal errors the vision has fallen. The European-trained philosophical critic might therefore say that Frye looks at literature from the point of view of the Hegelian end-state. It would seem to him as if Frye were replacing mystery with obscurity—unless he knew that Frye's analysis of error is identical with Blake's, and that his book on Blake, *Fearful Symmetry,* must be read in conjunction with the *Anatomy.*

The second topic of any historical inquiry, the authenticity of myth and of poetic language, is involved with religious doctrine. All disputes, for example, concerning the use of pagan or indeed

---

totle noted: the beginning, middle, and end. But by giving supreme attention to this temporal nature of drama we omit what, in Shakespeare, is at least of equivalent importance. A Shakespearian tragedy is set spatially as well as temporally in the mind. By this I mean that there are throughout the play a set of correspondences which relate to each other independently of the time-sequence which is the story. . . . Now if we are prepared to see the whole play laid out, so to speak, as an area, being simultaneously aware of these thickly-scattered correspondences in a single view of the whole, we possess the unique quality of the play in a new sense." From Knight's first chapter, "On the Priniciples of Shakespeare Interpretation."

any mythology in literature belong as much to the history of religion as of art. To resolve such disputes, scriptural and secular hermeneutics may differ in approach. The former depends almost totally on the principle of accommodation for its criterion of authenticity, but criticism is free to develop other criteria. Since Frye develops his own principle of accommodation, it may be useful to recall here the gist of the original doctrine.

It states that what is said or written may be a limiting form of what is meant, the limit being determined historically by the capacity of the hearers.[16] Interpretation, therefore, is essential not only to prevent wrong conclusions arising from the limiting form but also, in the presence of more capable hearers, to translate the intended thought into its true form. Criticism, however, as distinct from exegesis, may decide that the original form in its very concreteness or obscurity is more authentic than any supposed translation of it. Thus we often say that a metaphorical expression is not really translatable.

Frye's system reposes on a tacit assumption of the authenticity of myth, but we are in some difficulty if we ask how this authenticity is revealed. By what process do we accept the "Romantic" element in Shakespeare's comedies? According to Frye it is authenticated by being placed in a context of totality. The individual myth or isolated play reveals its archetypal features by the mutual association of a great number of works of art. What Frye pro-

---

[16] This does not imply that the speaker himself knows what is meant—he may be inspired, or the hermeneutic paradox which Dilthey emphasized may obtain, that we understand the author better than he understands himself. The speaker can be one of his hearers, sharing their limited historical situation.

poses is, in effect, a hermeneutic translation of literature into a clarified form, or "reconstructed mythology." Yet the absence of an official or dogmatic theology must always leave the authenticity of that form in doubt. Keats, for example, appreciated Romance and certainly understood the Romantic element in Shakespeare, yet felt like Wordsworth that the modern vocation was to surpass it. Myth, whether used substantively or merely as a narrative device, remains a problem for the Wordsworthian tradition. The literary counterpoint of mythical and secular in Eliot and others is a method reflecting this problematic yet insistent presence of myth.

There is, however, a concept in Frye which corresponds to the principle of accommodation and contributes to literary history because it reveals the difficult relation of poetic to ordinary discourse. I refer to what Frye calls displacement and defines as the "adaptation of myth and metaphor to canons of morality or plausibility." [17] So defined it is a restatement of the doctrine of accommodation. Frye supposes that there is such a thing as a pure myth (archetype) the displacements of which can be traced through history. The displacements have a specific direction which his first essay in the *Anatomy,* on Historical Criticism, describes. He there classifies all fiction in terms of the status of the hero who moves from a mythic or supernatural to an ironic or all-too-human mode of being. Thus Shakespeare's use of the Proserpine story shows a twofold displacement: as well as being an oblique version of the myth of death and revival, it had to be accommodated in Shakespeare's time to a "high mimetic" level of plausibility, i.e., it could no longer be a mythic story about gods, or a

[17] *Anatomy,* "Glossary," and cf. p. 136.

romantic fable, but only a tale of heroism in which the order of nature is not violated.

The concept of displacement enables us to revalue what grosser histories of literature see merely as secularization. For the movement from myth to realism does not infer the sad decline of hero into antihero or of an ancestor's great seal rings into Belinda's hairpin. We discover that secular man is not devoid of mythical attributes.[18] Except for Frye's hint of a cyclical return of realism to myth, the notion of displacement is empirically sound: it works; it is teachable; above all it reveals the permanence of Romance. One can no more remove the Romance element from art than natural instincts from man. It is eternal, as Freud discovered the instincts to be eternal, and therefore gave them the name of gods, Eros and Thanatos.

I suspect, however, that Frye has shown not that myth is displaced but that it is historical. It is never found in that unaccommodated state he posits when he mentions "the pure myth of death and revival" or when he claims that literature is a reconstructed mythology. One can make such a claim only by reducing myths to archetypes in the strictly Platonic sense of simples rather than complexes. But anyone who has read the *Anatomy* will agree that there are no simples in it. Or what simples there are, are hooked simples in the sense in which Lowes's *Road to Xanadu* explained Coleridge's fantastically assimilative mind by memories that are "hooked atoms." We do not find myth pure of religion or

18 So Hawthorne's Hester Prynne, Melville's Billy Budd, Hardy's Tess, and Mrs. Woolf's Septimus seem to assume the role of *pharmakos* or scapegoat—an observation carried into modern American fiction by Ihab Hassan's study of the "Radical Innocent."

literature; it comes to us institutionalized from the beginning, and though it may also be a body of structural principles there is no point in underplaying the war in the members of that body.

For, historically, some structural principles seem to exclude others: the realistic writer, as Frye notes, "finds that the requirements of literary form and plausible content always fight against each other. Just as the poetic metaphor is always a logical absurdity, so every inherited convention of plot in literature is more or less mad." [19] What is true of the realist is true of any writer, as Frye's own theory of displacement has shown: reality is never more than the *plausible* artifice. But in that case the notion of displacement becomes unnecessary except to indicate the direction of human credibility—credibility defining that realm in which contraries are no longer felt.

To Frye's total myth we must therefore add a historical account of the war that myth has waged with myth. Just as the redactors of the Book of Genesis had to reconcile several divergent formulas of the "myth" of creation, so it is in non-oral tradition: a writer does not confront a pure pattern, archetype, or convention, but a corpus of tales or principles that are far from harmonized. The pressure bringing unity out of diversity may indeed come from a latent archetype in the competing stories, but this raises the question of artistic unity—its necessary relation to a dialectical principle, such as the reconciliation of opposites or the harmonizing of variant traditions.

Temporality and authenticity are aspects, finally, of the largest topic of historical criticism: the relation of words to place of utterance. The metaphor of "situation," used several times in this

[19] "Myth, Fiction, and Displacement," *Fables of Identity,* p. 36.

essay, suggests that there is a determinable ground of presuppositions on which a writer stands consciously or unconsciously. Even the divine word, according to Angelus Silesius, could not exist without place—the world which it creates. "Der Ort und's Wort ist eins, und wäre nicht der Ort,/ Bei ewiger Ewigkeit! es wäre nicht das Wort." (Word and place are one, and if place did not exist/ By all that is eternal, the word could not exist.) The sense that art is addressed, that it is always in dialogue, is what historical criticism furthers.

Although Frye increases significantly our knowledge of the structural presuppositions of the literary work, he neglects the one presupposition which is most affected by place of origin: the verbal. He seems relatively unconcerned with the exact dialogue or status of words in the individual consciousness and the particular society. Such apt remarks, for example, as that Emily Dickinson's poetry was a form of personal correspondence ("This is my letter to the World") remain undeveloped or linked to theses on the general nature of poetry that diminish her peculiar paradox. Instead of examining "the verbal," Frye immediately subsumes it in what is called the "verbal universe." But this concept prevents a definitive description of the very element after which it is named.

For the concept of a verbal universe does not agree with what we know of the place of words in society. The opposition of science to art has always centered on the relation of words to things, which is another way of stating that words compete with conventions claiming to be better than verbal. Every writer *in* society is therefore concerned with the alternatives to the word. There has been fruitful conflict even among the arts themselves on the question of alternatives (musical, pictorial, hieroglyphic) to the verbal. This *paragone* may simply express the fact that all art aspires to the condition of totality; it remains, even so, a force in the writer's consciousness. Is there room in Frye's system— which has many chambers and not all opened—for that radical doubt, that innermost criticism which art brings to bear on itself? Or does his system circumvent the problematic character of verbal fictions?

Since the verbal, in Frye, is a larger category than the literary or the mythical, he may have intended to say that literature itself is always in dire need of being humanized. It becomes an institution easily infected by *ratio* and must be led back to its source in *oratio*. This surely is what the great work of fiction (or criticism) achieves: it recalls the origin of civilization in dialogic acts of naming, cursing, blessing, consoling, laughing, lamenting, and beseeching. These speak to us more openly than myth or archetype because they are the first-born children of the human voice. Myth and metaphor are endued with the acts, the gesta, of speech; and if there is a mediator for our experience of literature, it is something as simply with us as the human body, namely the human voice. It is here that one possibility of progress lies: in honoring the problematic relation of words to a reality they mediate rather than imitate. To envision "ghostlier demarcations" a poet must utter "keener sounds."

Thus Frye's criticism and a historical approach differ more than we are led to believe. Yet the reservations I have expressed should not be taken as a plea for conventional literary history, for that either does not face the question of the mission of art, or is content to show that art, like any cult or closed society, has a self-authenticating range of allusions to be decoded only by the priest of the cult: the historical expert.

## IV CRITICISM AND THE ORAL TRADITION

In conclusion, I recall ruefully Aristotle's remark that unity of plot does not consist in the unity of the hero. The plot was criticism, the hero Frye; and in case my reflections have been too picaresque, I would like to end with a firm and even didactic estimate of Frye's importance to contemporary criticism. The more we read in him the more we understand how essential the Romance tradition is, both in itself and in its modern afterlife. Poetry is inconceivable without it; even Shakespearean drama and the vast majority of novels conform to a Romance poetics, or are significantly clarified by it. Frye's permanent achievement is as a theorist whose recognitions favor Romance rather than Tragedy; and had he no more than rescued for us the spiritual form of William Blake, and then the spiritual form of Romance, it would have been sufficient.

Frye will not be grateful to me for considering him as the fulfillment of Bishop Hurd. And indeed he is much more, as I hope to have shown; yet his claim to provide the basis for a universal criticism remains less convincing than his Anatomy of Romance. His discoveries reflect on unity of design rather than unity of plot, and on the unity of art rather than the unity of the work of art. Even his style, a constant pleasure, is a Romance multiplication of recognitions and its symmetry an allegorical layering of the levels of recognition.

But this revival of a Romance poetics is of more than professional literary interest. It is Romance which mediated the themes and structures of the oral tradition; so that the revival of the one is linked to an interest in the other. Frye reverses the preference of Aristotle, who attempted to modify the predominance of oral tradition by esteeming unity of action more than the variegated energies of epic. The *Anatomy of Criticism* returns to the values implicit in the multiple design of Epic and Romance. The archetype as a structural principle resembles nothing so much as the *formula* of oral poetry, while Frye's system is in quest of a community as universal as that which oral poetry may have reached.

There is of course no question of a return to oral tradition. But there is some hope that its renewed appreciation will change our narrow concepts of originality in art, and permit us in reading a book to touch the central man and through him the life of generations. There is some hope that reading can become once more an encounter of imagination with imagination, as in Blake. But if Frye's purpose is to contribute to this encounter and to recover for literature its widest audience, his emphasis on system remains a stumbling block. Systems are the inkhorn children of bookcraft and erudition: they arise whenever humanists warm themselves on the ashes of myth. Despite Frye's return to a criticism nourished by the values of oral tradition, he has not escaped the ethos of the printed word. That "virile man standing in the sun" belongs to the Gutenberg Galaxy and is scanning the Milky Way of Romance as if it were an alienated part of his —and our—imagination. I cannot wish he were standing anywhere else or that he should descend to that "lower flight" which Raphael in *Paradise Lost* urged on Adam.

# Northrop Frye

\*

## *Reflections in a Mirror*

Reading critiques of oneself is normally a distressing pastime, ranking even below the rereading of one's own works. What variety one has usually seems to be multiplied in a wilderness of distorting mirrors. And if reading them is confusing, writing them almost affects one's sense of identity. Whatever has been published is grown up and has to make its own way in the world, preferably without further support from its parent. It is true that I have read these papers with an attention which at times amounts to pleasure, but their very excellence makes me wish that I could leave them to speak for themselves.

For I doubt if I can describe my ambitions for criticism more accurately than Mr. Fletcher does in his figure of the Haussmann boulevards which enabled Parisians, so to speak, to *see* Paris, or than Mr. Hartman does more conceptually in speaking of my wish to help demystify and democratize criticism. Mr. Hartman also notes in me a combination of interests which are partly scientific (perhaps the wrong word, though mine) and partly evangelical (certainly the right word, though not mine), the same mixture of detachment and engagement which exists in most areas of scholarship in the humanities. These two aims are contradictory, but as they are both essential, they have simply got to contradict: this is part of the paradox that Mr. Wimsatt speaks of as inherent in criticism. Both Mr. Fletcher and Mr. Hartman emphasize the fact that my work is designed to raise questions rather than answer them, and that my aim is not to construct a *Narrenschiff* to keep future critics all bound in by the same presuppositions, but to point to what Mr. Fletcher calls the open vistas and Mr. Hartman the still closed doors in the subject. A critic who has been compelled by such ambitions to write on far too broad a front is particularly vulnerable to objection on points of detail, but the errors and inconsistencies attributed to me by Mr. Wimsatt seldom seem to me to be really such, except on premises which are not mine. Given those premises, I do not appear to be misleading anybody very seriously, even myself. And even given Mr. Wimsatt's premises, it is clear that he finds much more than beautifully cadenced nonsense in me, otherwise he could hardly put his finger on so many central things: Plato's *Ion;* Oscar Wilde's *Decay of Lying* (which Messrs. Ellmann and Feidelson were quite right in putting at the beginning of their collection of documents of *The Modern Tradition*); the conception of poetry (not criticism) as a kind of forgery of myth.

When I began to work on Blake's Prophecies, it was constantly being said to me, both in books and in conversation:

"But even if you did provide a complete and self-consistent interpretation of their meaning, that wouldn't increase my interest in them as poetry." The phrase "as poetry" implies that the essence of poetry is somehow separable from its meaning, and the attitude underlying the statement was a value-judgment opposing itself to what I hoped would become a new body of critical knowledge. It seemed to me clear that the new knowledge had, as I put it later, a power of veto over the value-judgment: if the Prophecies could be shown to make sense, that would surely modify any view of them "as poetry." The critic's confidence in his value-judgment was, if he were an honest critic, admittedly tentative. He did not, however, as a rule, subordinate it to greater knowledge, but, like medieval princes fighting the Pope, he appealed to a future general council. Some day all such intuitions of value would be confirmed theoretically. This article of faith was usually expressed in an oracle of the type: "the end of criticism being evaluation, it is important to find trustworthy criteria of evaluation." I talked this way myself in an early version of the Polemical Introduction. But it became obvious that there were no such criteria, either in criticism or "elsewhere" (Mr. Bush's word quoted by Mr. Fletcher). It is true that my approach to criticism does not make any *functional* use of value-judgments: this has bewildered only the critics who have failed to notice that no criticism that actually gives us knowledge of literature, whether historical or linguistic or explicatory, does either. Perhaps a general council will yet meet and give us an apostolic creed of values, but in the meantime surely someone ought to make a simple and childish observation about the present nakedness of this venerable emperor. As I continued to work on Blake,

it became inescapably clear that the kind of thinking the Prophecies displayed was normal and typical poetic thinking, and that
every poet, from the first metaphor he uses, is condemned to
produce what Mr. Wimsatt calls Gnostic mythopoeia for the
rest of his poetic life.

"I must create a system," said Blake, and any critic going from
Blake into the general theory of criticism discovers how strong
and immediate the emotional overtones of the word "system"
are in this fragmented age. Jail-building, pigeonholing, providing
a glib answering service for undergraduates, overweening ambition on the part of the system-builder, are some of the readiest
associations. In the muddled mythology of stock response, the
system-builder is the spider who spins nets out of his bowels, as
contrasted with the bee who flits empirically from flower to
flower and staggers home under his burden of sweetness and
light. I have often said that I regard criticism itself as a systematic
subject, and there are systematic tendencies in the *Anatomy of
Criticism,* particularly in the way that it tries to unite different
critical methods, putting Mr. Wimsatt into what he calls a wintry
cellar, though it might also be called a ratproof foundation. But
I do not think of the *Anatomy* as primarily systematic: I think
of it rather as schematic. The reason why it is schematic is that
poetic thinking is schematic. The structure of images that C. S.
Lewis in *The Discarded Image* calls "the Model" was a projected
schematic construct which provided the main organization for
literature down to the Renaissance: it modulated into less projected forms after Newton's time, but it did not lose its central
place in literature. The attraction that poets have felt during the
last two centuries for occult and other offbeat forms of thought,

while very largely ignoring the advance of real science, has always seemed to me an instructive example of the affinity to pattern-making schematism which is part of the poetic process itself. The *Anatomy,* especially in its third essay, attempts to provide an outline of a schema which, as I said, I hoped would serve as a guide to practical criticism. It is not a view of the universe, whether true or fictional, and it is not a reconstruction of any specific pattern in the past. It employs four seasons because that is the most convenient number for such a schema to have, not because I am unaware that "sumer is icumen in" means "spring is here." Since the book appeared, I have received enough correspondence echoing Mr. Hartman's "it works; it is teachable" to make me reasonably satisfied with its general usefulness.

In the last few years I have become more preoccupied with the context of criticism in education, and I think I understand, more clearly than I did ten years ago, why so many critics actually prefer that their subject should be theoretically addled. The "mystique" that Mr. Hartman mentions is certainly important here: I think that there is also another element derived from the classroom. In Mr. Trilling's recent book there is a penetrating essay on the way in which the study of modern literature seems to have the odd effect of denaturing it. We recognize Rimbaud or Kafka or Lawrence or Dostoievsky as great writers because of a tremendous force of passion and power and clairvoyance that comes through them, a force so great, and carrying an anguish so unbearable, that we are not surprised to find it crippling their lives with neurosis and perversity. What such writers may incidentally have done or said does not matter: the insight is what matters, and we are anxious to confront our students with the insight, purified of the accidents of temperament. The result is that the students write more or less competent essays about the passion, power, anguish, etc., of these authors and go on about their business, while the teacher is in the position of saying, like a chairman at a lecture, "I am sure we are all deeply grateful to Mr. Rimbaud (and the others) for having contributed such a distinctive note to our understanding of human life." There is no way out of this: for better or worse, criticism is part of an educational process in which *Macbeth* is taught to children, and in which a certain insulation against emotional impact is a sign of cultivated taste. Teachers are occupationally disposed to believe in magic, and it is not surprising that many of them should cherish the illusion that they are best able to charge their students' batteries directly with the authors they teach if they do not admit, even to themselves, that all teaching is a transposition of literature into criticism, of passion and power and anguish into pattern and craftsmanship and the following of convention. If, that is, they can keep on assuming that the direct experience of literature can somehow be, if not actually taught, at least communicated.

Hence, perhaps, the resistance to attempts in criticism to make the resemblances and recurring patterns in the variety of literary experience significant. I am often told that this detracts from the distinctiveness of the work of literature, this quality being expanded into a value only by rhetorical license, the world's worst poem being obviously as distinctive as the best. It is as though a zoologist were to insist that the differences between mastiffs and chihuahuas made the conception "dog" a useless pedantry. Mr. Wimsatt, who is not normally this sentimental kind of critic, describes my own recurring patterns as clichés, meaning apparently that, even if the connections are there, it is bad form to call attention to them.

Mr. Ransom's conception of "texture" is one from which every critic has learned a great deal, but his view that structure, which means ultimately the study of such recurring principles of literature as convention and genre, is somehow less relevant to criticism, is something I have never understood. The principle that a work of literature should not be related to anything outside itself is sound enough, but I cannot see how the rest of literature can be regarded as outside the work of literature, any more than the human race can be regarded as outside a human being. When I use the metaphor of standing back from a work of literature, as one would from a painting, to see the structural principles in it, I am trying to give some reality to the word "literature," by placing the reader in the middle of that great museum without walls which Mr. Hartman has so well described as the form of understanding appropriate to our time, when technology has both unified and decentralized our relation to works of art. If Mr. Wimsatt asks who really wants to see a painting in that way, the answer is, everybody interested in twentieth-century painting, abstract expressionism being only the most dramatic of several contemporary modes of painting from precisely this perspective. Mr. Fletcher is right in connecting my interest in comedy and in utopian forms with my interest in literature as a total community, where every resemblance is a recognition scene. Such recognition scenes are, as a rule, both sublime and ridiculous, a fact which largely accounts for what Mr. Fletcher calls the low comedy of my style. This is partly because parody of convention is as frequent as taking it straight. It seems to me worth notice that the opening sentences of *Pride and Prejudice* and of *Anna Karenina* are in a convention of beginning a story with a sententious statement which goes back at least to medieval rhetoric. But the fact that this convention is being used ironically, with a playful irony in one and a savage irony in the other, is equally obvious. Other recognition scenes, such as the conventional romance pattern of the cave episode which helps to establish the literary context of *Tom Sawyer,* seem quasi-ridiculous to those who are unaccustomed or unwilling to think in terms of literary context. They are "irrelevant" (Mr. Wimsatt's word) only if the word "literature" is meaningless. And if it is meaningless, criticism is not a very significant subject.

Such persisting conventions come down from the past, and from one point of view my emphasis on recurring structural principles seems to go back in the past until it disappears into that inaccessible powder-room of the Muses, prehistoric mythology. For the way in which the recurring structural elements of literature (convention, genre, archetype) are held together by and in myth, I must refer the reader to the *Anatomy of Criticism*. I speak of an early mythical period of literature because it seems clear that there was such a period. But nobody can catch literature in the act of originating, and in one sense it is even illogical to speak of "a" myth at all except for convenience. We cannot really think of a myth apart from a specific verbal embodiment of that myth, just as we cannot think of a sonata in music apart from the embodiment of the sonata form in actual compositions. It is not the antiquity of myth but its permanence that makes it a structural principle of literature: not the wisdom hidden behind the story of Endymion but the art revealed, explicitly in Drayton and Lyly and Keats, implicitly in hundreds of other stories and poems that are based on the Endymion theme. I know that portentous language is often used about myths, and similar sound effects have been attributed to the *Anatomy* by Mr. Wimsatt, following Mr. Abrams; but they are not there. And if they were, a few woo-woo noises about the hoary antiquity of myths would be trifling enough compared to the dismal and illiberal impoverishment of literary experience that results from ignoring the structure into which that experience enters. It is only the individual and discrete literary experience that melts "into thin air": what does not vanish is the total vision which contains the experience.

Hence when I say that Shakespearean comedy demands a primitive response, I am not saying that our response should be similar to that of a hypothetical noble savage. My example of a primitive response is taken from *Pamela:* it could just as well have been taken from Dickens or Tolstoi. By a primitive response I mean an unmediated response, a response that is neither naïve, like Partridge's response to *Hamlet* in *Tom Jones,* nor so sophisticated as to be indifferent, but is the kind of direct response to the power of literature which is only possible when one stands inside the structure of literature, and is neither confusing it with life nor building an emotional barricade against it. Here we come back to our classroom problem, where we find that exposing students to anguish and nausea leads only to notes and essays about anguish and nausea. This situation grows out of an earlier one in which the student's unmediated responses are to his comic books and television programs, while his response to *Macbeth* has every conceivable kind of inhibition attached to it.

When I urge the early study of biblical and classical myths, it is because I am in search of a literary curriculum that will not only make sense as a discipline, but, by building up the sense of a literary order and putting the student inside it, will be directly concerned with developing a response of this kind, where genuine literature has the kind of effect that popular literature has now (popular is always more or less a synonym for primitive for me). It is the belief in the possibility of such response, derived from their own experience of it, that keeps teachers of English going in their often discouraging calling.

Recently a writer referred to my views on literary education as a contribution to the climate of opinion which is trying to rationalize American imperialism in Vietnam. The associative links in this argument elude me, but I can dimly glimpse one point, and it is the only point that occurs to me as a comment on the last part of Mr. Hartman's paper. As Mr. Fletcher emphasizes, my own bias is naturally a historical one, but I have never been very clear about the shape of the history of literature apart from the shape of history in general. I know that there is a complicated interplay between a work of literature and its time, and one which is far more important than the dreary kind of "background" criticism which is written on the principle of Walt Disney's *Fantasia* a generation ago, where a visual barrage of Gothic arches and the like was supposed to relieve the tedium of listening to a Bach toccata. But the only shaping principles of history in literature itself that I have dealt with, as Mr. Hartman says, are those of displacement, the oscillating of technique from the stylizing of form to the manifesting of content and back again, and of what I call existential projection, the attributing of poetic schematism to the objective world, which takes different forms in different historical epochs. I have even compared the literary universe to Blake's Beulah, where no dispute can come, where everything is equally an element of a liberal education, where Bunyan and Rochester are met together and Jane Austen and the Marquis de Sade have kissed each other. This is not the way that works of literature enter history, and it is quite possible that the wars of myth in time are an aspect of criticism that I have not grasped. But one form of this historical war I think I do understand.

Myth is liberated by literature, but it also works in society as a reactionary force, providing for prejudice and stock response what vision they have, producing what Mr. Wimsatt calls the cliché, the literary formula that ought not to be repeated. Literature has the pastoral; social mythology has the cottage away from it all or the nostalgia for the world of one's childhood. Literature has the quest; social mythology has the gospel of getting on. Literature has comedy; social mythology goes out to win friends and influence people. But, as these examples have already made clear, social mythology has its own kind of literature. The question of evaluation in criticism is thus not a matter of individual appraisal, as one would appraise the value of a diamond or a piece of antique furniture; it is part of a social and moral struggle, of what Ionesco, making an essential distinction that Mr. Wimsatt misses, calls the opposition of archetypes to stereotypes. All my educational views are based on this opposition, and have as their aim the attempt to win for literature the response generally given to social mythology. Whether we find them in literature or in the verbal formulas of ordinary life, myths constitute the vision that the individual man has of the human situation. But within these myths a dialectical struggle shapes up between the tendency in man merely to accept what is handed him from his environment and the effort to choose and control his vision. Those who have really changed the modern world—Rousseau, Freud, Marx —are those who have changed its mythology, and whatever is beneficent in their influence has to do with giving man increased power over his own vision. In the continuation of this struggle literary criticism has a central role, and if I can do anything to forward it I shall be quite content to be called the fulfillment of Bishop Hurd.

For it was Hurd who established the principle of the unity of design in criticism. Anybody can see an infinite number of exquisite touches of human nature in Shakespearean comedy, of lovely passages in Spenser, of brilliant realistic effects in Chaucer, but somehow the over-all structure of their works seems quite different, something which by comparison, if we keep to the same standards, seems absurd, unnatural, or fantastic. Hurd's principle helps us to see how the exquisite details exist, not in spite of a fantastic and incredible design, but because of it. Similarly, the exquisite and lucid lyrics of Blake could not have been written except from within the kind of mental structure that emerges more consciously in the often deplored Prophecies. Even on my own level I find from experience that something similar is true. Many who consider the structure of my view of literature repellent find useful parenthetic insights in me, but the insights would not be there unless the structure were there too. So I deduce that such readers are fitting these insights into over-all structures of their own, though they may be less conscious of possessing them. What can be communicated, in this situation, is the insights themselves together with a challenge to clarify their new context.

There is thus an objective mythical structure, which is the world of literature itself, and which criticism as a whole seeks to articulate, and a subjective one, which the student achieves as a result of his literary experience. The objective structure must be as schematic as the study itself demands, but the subjective one is less obviously so. We think of the vertebrate as a higher organization than the crustacean: what articulates the cultivated and disciplined mind tends to become increasingly invisible. This does not mean that the student outgrows the systematic presentation of literature in criticism: it means that his goal is a personal vision which includes literature but is greater in scope. The mythical structure of literature is not this vision, but it is the only way of getting to it. Literature is not ultimately objective: it is not simply there, like nature: it is there to serve mankind. In Wallace Stevens' poem "Lytton Strachey, Also, Enters into Heaven," Strachey realizes that something he identifies with a new perception of myth lies ahead of him as the fulfillment of what his intense but very limited rationalism was pointing to:

> Perception as an act of intelligence
> And perception as an act of grace
> Are two quite different things, in particular
> When applied to the mythical.

What is demanded from him is an expansion of perception through the "properly misunderstood" myth into an understanding, and this requires a good many extra qualities, including, somewhat unexpectedly, a new kind of courage. He shrinks from this, and settles for a quiet quarter in heaven, "Dixhuitième and Georgian and serene," when he could have had the whole city for his possession.

The real Lytton Strachey knew what he wanted, and the fact that in Stevens' heaven he does not get what he does not want is hardly significant in itself. But it would be a disaster if the failure of nerve that Stevens portrays in this poem became a cultural phenomenon of our time, and a disaster of much more than literary importance. Mythology is curiously like technology in its development: the more man invents of it, the more strongly tempted he is to project it into something that controls him. The immense pressure toward conformity in thought and imagination is society's anxious response to mythopoeia, creating institutional religion in one age and total political alignments in another. No one person, certainly not one critic, can kill this dragon who guards our word-hoard, but for some of us, at any rate, there can be no question of going back to our secluded Georgian quarters, from which serenity has long since disappeared.

# John E. Grant

*

# A Checklist of Writings
# by and about Northrop Frye

For more than fifteen years I have admired Mr. Frye's work and incidentally kept track of notices which his work received, but I had not thought of compiling a systematic list until I was asked by Mr. Krieger to do so in November, 1965. Inevitably a checklist so rapidly put together will be found to contain lacunae, though I hope I have not overlooked many important items. The time and library resources available made it impossible for me to read or reread every item in order to check its reliability, but I am confident that most of the data are accurate. Let me begin, however, by soliciting corrections and additions.

This Checklist could not have been completed had it not been for the kind cooperation of Mr. Frye and of the American and British publishers of his books. Mr. Frye provided his personal list of publications through November 1, 1965, and I was able to add only a few items, apart from reprint data, to this list. Two features of the first part of the Checklist require some comment. Mr. Frye chose to group his writings as they are listed here, that is, according to the various media of publication and then chronologically within each group. While no better way of presenting so large and various a body of work suggested itself, this system has the disadvantage that, whenever a new item, for example, a book, is published, the number assigned to each subsequent item in the Checklist must be changed. I have allayed this problem temporarily by entering several items scheduled for 1966 publication, though it is possible that they may not appear on time. Furthermore, since Mr. Frye's work is by no means at an end, I regret having to employ a system of numbering which tends to imply that it is. The instability of item numbers will also quickly render obsolescent my Subject Index to Mr. Frye's writings, but I believe that the Index will assist the reader to recognize the scope and variety of Frye's work as a whole, even though it must represent *Fearful Symmetry* as being merely a book about Blake.

The other feature concerns the absence of technical detail in the Checklist. Of periodicals mentioned in Sections D, E, and F only the date of publication, rather than the volume number, is given. Mr. Frye chose to provide only this information on his own list and I could think of no sufficient reason for looking up all these inert data concerning volume numbers. For consistency's sake it also seemed best to follow the same practice in Part II of the Checklist.

For the second part I had no previous master list to work from, but Mr. Frye's publishers were very helpful in promptly providing Xerox copies of reviews in their possession. Unfortunately, however, their files were seldom complete and they contained inaccuracies, which left me with much to do. Such assistance as I was able to derive from the *Reader's Guide* or the *International Index* served chiefly to remind me how inadequate are the present data-collecting media in the humanities. While my charge was to produce an enumerative rather than a descriptive (let alone an evaluative) list, I observed that significant reviews are often not listed anywhere. Fortunately, there was just time to make a few inquiries, and I am grateful to Hazard Adams, Michael Platt, Compton Rees, and Herbert Weil, who were able to point out items that might have escaped my notice. Mr. Frye's research assistant, Miss Jay Macpherson, was also exceptionally helpful in calling my attention to Canadian notices that I would otherwise not have discovered.

It seemed most useful to arrange notices chronologically according to the book being discussed. This arrangement is less satisfactory than an alphabetical master list in so far as it is not as easy to see at a glance whether a certain critic has commented on several books. There are also a few portmanteau reviews of several volumes, but only in those of Eli Mandel in the *Tamarack Review,* 1963, and William Blissett in the *University of Toronto Quarterly,* 1964, are a number of books taken up seriatim; therefore these are the only notices which are repeated for several books. The arrangement I finally chose has the distinct advantage of indicating something of the growth of Mr. Frye's reputation; moreover, the number of notices is not yet so great that the reader cannot scan and quickly find the name of whatever critic interests him. It seemed unwise to assign numbers to the various notices in Part II because they might become confused with the items in Part I. In a few instances my information was incomplete and the title (if it has one), issue, or pagination of a review is not included. An incomplete reference seems obviously preferable to none at all.

In the cases of *Fearful Symmetry* and *Anatomy of Criticism* additional lists of notable books that contain Frye entries in their indices have been provided, but I have given the number of pages on which Frye is referred to rather than a transcription of the indices. When journal articles have subsequently been incorporated into books, I have included only the book references. This will tend to obscure a little the picture of the emergence of Mr. Frye's reputation, but a lean list is more appropriate for present purposes than a fat one. Moreover, the publication dates of the books in question can only indicate approximate termini for Blake criticism and literary theory respectively. Even before *Anatomy of Criticism* appeared, Mr. Frye's theories had been carefully considered by Messrs. Crane, Davie, and Wimsatt and Brooks, and his work and reputation as a Blakeist is still in progress.

I have not made a systematic search for reviews in newspapers and have ordinarily included only pieces of some weight and seriousness. But enough references in nonscholarly periodicals have come to my attention to justify including references to some whose concern is "life" rather than scholarship. Inevitably part of the interest of such a list as this one is sociological rather than intellectual. While this selective policy encourages a partisan compiler to suppress references to material he disagrees with, I have never intentionally done so. Indeed, though the standard of criticism of Mr. Frye's work has been remarkably high, a few lengthy items are listed which are less competent than the ephemera in *Publisher's Weekly* and the like which have been omitted. But if any significant notice is not included the reason is that I have overlooked it rather than that I disagree with it.

Originally I had thought that I might increase the usefulness of this Checklist without departing from the spirit of my charge to be merely enumerative if I were to indicate whether each notice is either favorable, unfavorable, or mixed. But it became clear that such a division of the material would at times be more misleading than helpful. Especially in the case of *Anatomy of Criticism* many intricately mixed opinions have been expressed. Some critics have judged the book to be a brilliant performance in itself but useless or even pernicious in its influence, while others have pronounced it to be frequently illuminating or useful but theoretically unsound. An extreme considered reaction is that of J. F. Kermode, who declared that, though *Anatomy of Criticism* is the most important work of literary criticism published in the last decade, it is nevertheless "entirely wrong." Mr. Kermode's entire statement is only a few sentences long, but such judgments reveal the futility of attempting to reduce a complex idea to a sign. At this point the compiler is reminded that he has done what he can and should turn to more substantive work.

## 1. A Checklist of Frye's Writings

*Note:* This list does not include:

(a) a number of brief reviews
(b) unpublished speeches or scripts written for the Canadian Broadcasting Company or the National Film Board

(c) unsigned writings (contributions to committee reports, editorials for the *Canadian Forum,* etc.)

(d) routine university writing (citations, contributions, to *Victoria Reports, Varsity Graduate,* etc.)

(e) contributions to encyclopedias

A. BOOKS PUBLISHED

1. *Fearful Symmetry: A Study of William Blake.* Princeton, Princeton University Press, 1947. 462 pp. Reprinted, paperback edition, 1958. Reprinted, paperback edition, with a new preface, Boston, Beacon Press, 1962.

2. *Anatomy of Criticism: Four Essays.* Princeton, Princeton University Press, 1957. 383 pp. Reprinted. Portions reprinted in a number of books.*

* The following have come to my attention: "The Structure of Comedy," in *Eight Great Comedies,* ed. Sylvan Barnet, Morton Berman, and William Burto, pp. 461–69 (New York, 1958); "Specific Forms of Drama," in *The Study of Literature: A Handbook of Critical Essays and Terms,* ed. Sylvan Barnet, Morton Berman, and William Burto, pp. 139–52 (Boston, 1960); "The Four Forms of Fiction," in *Discussions of the Novel,* ed. Roger Sale, pp. 3–11 (Boston, 1960); "Fictional Modes" (abridged) and "Specific Continuous Forms," in *Approaches to the Novel: Materials for a Poetics,* ed. Robert Scholes, pp. 31–37 and 41–54 (San Francisco, 1961); "Anagogic Phase: The Symbol as Monad," in *Modern Criticism: Theory and Practice,* ed. Walter Sutton and Richard Foster, pp. 296–303 (New York, 1962); "The Mythos of Winter: Irony and Satire," in *Modern Satire,* ed. Alvin Kernan, pp. 155–64 (New York, 1962); "The Structure of Comedy," in *Aspects of Drama: A Handbook,* ed. Sylvan Barnet, Morton Berman, and William Burto, pp. 70–80 (Boston, 1962); "Specific Forms of Drama," in *The Context and Craft of Drama,* ed. Robert W. Corrigan and James L.

2a. *Analyse der Literaturkritik.* Translated by Edgar Lohner and Henning Clewing. Stuttgart, Kohlhammer, 1964. 380 pp.

2b. Italian translation in preparation.

2c. Paperback edition, New York, Atheneum Press, 1966.

3. *The Well-Tempered Critic.* The Page-Barbour Lectures, University of Virginia. Bloomington, Indiana University Press, 1963. 160 pp.

4. *The Educated Imagination.* The Massey Lectures, Canadian Broadcasting Corporation. Toronto, 1963. 68 pp. Hard-cover and paperback. Reprinted, hard-cover and paperback editions, Bloomington, Indiana University Press, 1964. 156 pp.

5. *T. S. Eliot.* Writers and Critics Series. Edinburgh, Oliver and Boyd, 1963. 106 pp.

6. *Fables of Identity: Studies in Poetic Mythology.* New York, Harcourt, Brace and World, 1963. 265 pp. Reprint of Nos. 32, 33, 34, 36, 37, 39, 72, 80, 97, 98, 100, 101, 105, 108, 109, and 146. Hard-cover and paperback.

7. *A Natural Perspective: The Development of Shakespearean Comedy and Romance.* The Bampton Lectures in America. New York, Columbia University Press, 1965. 159 pp.

8. *The Return of Eden: Five Essays on Milton's Epics.* The Huron College Centennial Lectures, with a revised version of No. 95. Toronto, University of Toronto Press, 1965. 143 pp.

---

Rosenberg, pp. 214–27 (San Francisco, 1964); "Theory of Genres," in *Perspectives on Epic,* ed. Frederick H. Candelaria and William C. Strange, pp. 114–20 (Boston, 1965).

9. John Milton, *Paradise Lost and Selected Poetry and Prose.* Introduction and Notes. Rinehart Editions. New York, 1951. xxxviii + 601 pp.

10. Pelham Edgar, *Across My Path.* Edited with an Introduction. Toronto, 1952. xi + 167 pp. Introduction, pp. vii–xi.

11. William Blake, *Selected Poetry and Prose.* Edited with an Introduction. A Modern Library Book. New York, 1953. xxx + 475 pp.

12. C. T. Currelly, *I Brought the Ages Homes.* Edited with an Introduction. Toronto, 1956. x + 312 pp. Introduction, pp. vii–x.

13. *Sound and Poetry.* English Institute Essays, 1956. New York, 1957. xxvii + 156 pp. Preface, pp. v–vi, and Introduction ("Lexis and Melos"), pp. ix–xxviii.

14. E. J. Pratt, *Collected Poems* (2d ed.). Edited with an Introduction. Toronto, 1958. xxviii + 395 pp. Introduction, pp. xiii–xxviii.

15. Shakespeare, *The Tempest.* Introduction and Notes. The Pelican Shakespeare. General Editor: Alfred Harbage. Penguin Books. Baltimore, Md., 1959. 112 pp. Introduction, pp. 15–26.

16. Thomas McCulloch, *The Stepsure Letters.* (Originally published as *Letters of Mephibosheth Stepsure.*) Edited with an

Introduction. New Canadian Library. Toronto, 1960. ix +
160 pp. Introduction, pp. iii–ix.

17. Peter F. Fisher, *The Valley of Vision: Blake as Prophet and
Revolutionary*. Edited with an Introduction. Toronto, 1961.
xi + 261 pp. "Editor's Preface," pp. v–vii.

18. *Design for Learning*. Reports submitted to the Joint Committee of the Toronto Board of Education and the University
of Toronto. Edited with an Introduction. Toronto, 1962. x +
148 pp. Introduction, pp. 3–17.

19. *Romanticism Reconsidered*. English Institute Essays, 1962.
Edited with a foreword. New York, 1963. ix + 144 pp. Foreword, pp. v–ix. (See also No. 42.)

20. *Blake: A Collection of Critical Essays*. Twentieth Century
Views Series. Edited with an Introduction. Englewood Cliffs,
N.J., 1966. 183 pp. Introduction, pp. 1–7. (See also Nos. 82 and
102.)

(51. Joint editorship.)


c. Contributions to Books

21. "The Argument of Comedy," in *English Institute Essays
1948,* ed. Alan Downer, pp. 58–73. New York, 1949. Reprinted in *Shakespeare: Modern Essays in Criticism,* ed.
Leonard F. Dean, pp. 79–89. New York, 1957. Also in *Comedy: Plays, Theory, and Criticism,* ed. Marvin Felheim, pp.
236–41. New York, 1962. Also in *Theories of Comedy,* ed.
Paul Lauter, pp. 449–60. Garden City, N.Y., 1964. Also in

*Shakespeare's Twelfth Night,* ed. Leonard F. Dean and James A. S. McPeak, pp. 93–101. Boston, 1965.

22. "The Church: Its Relation to Society," in *The Living Church,* ed. H. W. Vaughan, pp. 152–72. Toronto, 1949.

23. "Blake's Treatment of the Archetype," in *English Institute Essays 1950,* ed. Alan Downer, pp. 170–96. New York, 1951. Reprinted in *Discussions of William Blake,* ed. John E. Grant, pp. 6–16. Boston, 1961.

24. "Trends in Modern Culture," in *The Heritage of Western Culture,* ed. R. C. Chalmers, pp. 102–17. Toronto, 1952.

25. "Oswald Spengler," in *Architects of Modern Thought,* Canadian Broadcasting Corporation, 1st Series, pp. 83–90. Toronto, 1955.

26. "William Blake," in *The English Romantic Poets and Essayists: A Review of Research and Criticism,* ed. C. W. and L. H. Houtchens, pp. 1–31. New York, 1957. Revised and updated by Martin K. Nurmi in a new edition. New York, 1966.

27. "Notes for a Commentary on *Milton,*" in *The Divine Vision: Studies in the Poetry and Art of William Blake,* ed. V. de S. Pinto, pp. 97–137. London, 1957.

28. "Preface to an Uncollected Anthology," in *Studia Varia,* ed. E. G. D. Murray for the Royal Society of Canada, pp. 21–36. Toronto, 1957.

29. "Poetry," in *The Arts in Canada,* ed. Malcolm Ross, pp. 84–90. Toronto, 1958.

30. "Sir James Frazer," in *Architects of Modern Thought,* Canadian Broadcasting Corporation, 3d and 4th Series, pp. 22–32. Toronto, 1959.

31. "Religion and Modern Poetry," in *Challenge and Response: Modern Ideas and Religion,* ed. R. C. Chalmers and John A. Irving, pp. 23–36. Toronto, 1959.

32. "Literature as Context: Milton's *Lycidas,*" in *Comparative Literature,* Vol. I (Proceedings of the International Comparative Literature Association at the University of North Carolina), ed. W. P. Friederich, pp. 44–55. Chapel Hill, 1959. Reprinted in *Milton's Lycidas: The Tradition and the Poem,* ed. C. A. Patrides, pp. 200–211. New York, 1961.

33. "George Gordon, Lord Byron," in *Major British Writers,* Vol. II, Enlarged edition, G. B. Harrison, General Editor, pp. 149–234. New York, 1959. Introduction and Selection (Notes included).

34. "New Directions from Old," in *Myth and Myth-Making,* ed. Henry A. Murray, pp. 115–31. New York, 1960. Reprinted in *The Making of Myth,* ed. Richard M. Ohmann, pp. 66–82. New York, 1962.

35. "The Critical Discipline," in *Canadian Universities Today,* ed. George Stanley and Guy Sylvestre for the Royal Society of Canada, pp. 30–37. Toronto, 1961. Reprinted (with some additions and alterations) in *The Aims of Education,* ed. Freeman K. Stewart for the Canadian Conference on Education (Conference Study No. 1), pp. 24–32. Ottawa, 1961.

36. "Emily Dickinson," in *Major Writers of America,* Vol. II,

Perry Miller, General Editor, pp. 3–46. New York, 1962. Introduction and Selection (Notes included).

37. "How True a Twain," in *The Riddle of Shakespeare's Sonnets,* pp. 25–53. New York, 1962.

38. "Shakespeare's Experimental Comedy," "The Tragedies of Nature and Fortune," "Proposal of Toast," in *Stratford Papers on Shakespeare 1961,* ed. B. W. Jackson, pp. 2–14, 38–55, 195–96. Toronto, 1962.

39. "Recognition in *The Winter's Tale,*" in *Essays on Shakespeare and Elizabethan Drama: In Honor of Hardin Craig,* ed. Richard Hosley, pp. 235–46. Columbia, Mo., 1962.

40. "The Developing Imagination," in *Learning in Language and Literature,* pp. 38–62. Cambridge, Mass., 1963. (The Inglis Lecture.)

41. "The Road of Excess," in *Myth and Symbol: Critical Approaches and Applications,* ed. Bernice Slote, pp. 3–20. Lincoln, 1963.

42. "The Drunken Boat: The Revolutionary Element in Romanticism," in *Romanticism Reconsidered* (see No. 19), pp. 1–25. New York, 1963.

43. "Literary Criticism," in *The Aims and Methods of Scholarship in Modern Languages and Literatures,* ed. James Thorpe, pp. 57–69. New York, 1963.

44. "Preface," in *The Psychoanalysis of Fire,* pp. v–viii. By Gaston Bachelard. Translated by A. C. M. Ross. Boston, 1963.

45. "The Problem of Spiritual Authority in the Nineteenth Century," in *Literary Views: Critical and Historical Essays,* ed.

Carroll Camden, pp. 145–58. Chicago, 1964. Reprinted, with some alterations, in *Essays in English Literature from the Renaissance to the Victorian Age Presented to A. S. P. Woodhouse,* ed. Miller MacLure and Frank W. Watt, pp. 304–19. Toronto, 1964.

46. "Conclusion," in *A Literary History of Canada,* ed. Carl Klinck and others, pp. 821–49. Toronto, 1965.

47. "Foreword," in *Prospects of Change: Proposals for Canada's Future,* ed. Abraham Rotstein, pp. xiii–xv. Toronto, 1965.

48. "Nature and Nothing," in *Essays on Shakespeare,* ed. Gerald W. Chapman, pp. 35–58. Princeton, 1965.

49. "The Structure and Spirit of Comedy," in *Stratford Papers on Shakespeare,* ed. B. W. Jackson, pp. 1–9. Toronto, 1965.

50. "The Rising of the Moon: A Study of Yeats's Vision," in *An Honoured Guest: New Essays on W. B. Yeats,* ed. Denis Donoghue and J. R. Mulryne. London, 1966.

51. "The Keys of the Gates," in *Some British Romantics: A Collection of Essays,* ed. James V. Logan, John E. Jordan, and Northrop Frye. Columbus, Ohio, 1966.

52. "Reflections in a Mirror," in *Northrop Frye in Modern Criticism,* English Institute Essays, 1965, ed. Murray Krieger. New York, 1966.

D. PERIODICAL ARTICLES

53. "The Jooss Ballet," *Canadian Forum,* April, 1936, p. 18.

54. "Wyndham Lewis," *Canadian Forum,* June, 1936, p. 21.

55. "Frederick Delius," *Canadian Forum,* August, 1936, p. 19.

56. "Music and the Savage Breast," *Canadian Forum,* April, 1938, p. 451.

57. "Men as Trees Walking," *Canadian Forum,* October, 1938, p. 208. (On a surrealist exhibition.)

58. "Canadian Art in London," *Canadian Forum,* January, 1939, p. 304.

59. "Canadian and Colonial Painting," *Canadian Forum,* March, 1940.

60. "Canadian Watercolors," *Canadian Forum,* April, 1940, p. 14.

61. "War on the Cultural Front," *Canadian Forum,* August, 1940, p. 144.

62. "The Great Charlie," *Canadian Forum,* August, 1941, pp. 148–50. (On Chaplin's *Great Dictator.*)

63. "Music in Poetry," *University of Toronto Quarterly,* January, 1942, pp. 166–79.

64. "The Anatomy in Prose Fiction," *The Manitoba Arts Review,* Spring, 1942, pp. 35–47.

65. "Reflections at a Movie," *Canadian Forum,* October, 1942, pp. 212–13.

66. "Music in the Movies," *Canadian Forum,* December, 1942, p. 275.

67. "Water Colour Annual," *Canadian Art,* June–July, 1944, pp. 187–89.

68. "The Nature of Satire," *University of Toronto Quarterly,*

October, 1944, pp. 75–89. Reprinted in *Satire: Theory and Practice,* ed. Charles A. Allen and George D. Stephens, pp. 15–30. Belmont, Calif., n.d. [1962].

69. "A Liberal Education," *Canadian Forum,* Part I, September, 1945, p. 134; Part II, October, 1945, p. 162.

70. "La tradition narrative dans la poésie canadienne-anglais," *Gants du Ciel,* Spring, 1946, pp. 19–30. (French translation by Guy Sylvestre.)

71. "Education and the Humanities," *United Church Observer,* August 1, 1947, p. 5.

72. "Yeats and the Language of Symbolism," *University of Toronto Quarterly,* October, 1947, pp. 1–17.

73. "The Eternal Tramp," *Here and Now 1,* December, 1947, pp. 8–11. (On Chaplin's *Monsieur Verdoux:* title supplied by the editor.)

74. "David Milne: An Appreciation," *Here and Now 2,* May, 1948, pp. 47–48. (Illustrated.)

75. "Dr. Kinsey and the Dream Censor," *Canadian Forum,* July, 1948, pp. 85–86.

76. "The Pursuit of Form," *Canadian Art,* Christmas, 1948, pp. 54–57. (On Lawren Harris.)

77. "The Function of Criticism at the Present Time," *University of Toronto Quarterly,* October, 1949, pp. 1–16. Reprinted in *Our Sense of Identity: A Book of Canadian Essays,* ed. Malcolm Ross, pp. 247–65. Toronto, 1954.

78. "The Four Forms of Prose Fiction," *Hudson Review,* Win-

ter, 1950, pp. 582–95. Reprinted in *The Hudson Review Anthology,* ed. Frederick Morgan, pp. 336–50. New York, 1961.

79. "Levels of Meaning in Literature," *Kenyon Review,* Spring, 1950, pp. 246–62.

80. "The Archetypes of Literature" (No. VII of "My Credo"), *Kenyon Review,* Winter, 1951, pp. 92–110. Reprinted in *Myth and Method: Modern Theories of Fiction,* ed. James E. Miller, Jr., pp. 144–62. Lincoln, 1960.

81. "Poetry" (Letters in Canada 1950), *University of Toronto Quarterly,* April, 1951, pp. 257–61.

82. "Poetry and Design in William Blake," *Journal of Aesthetics and Art Criticism,* September, 1951, pp. 35–43. Reprinted in *Discussions of William Blake,* ed. John E. Grant, pp. 44–49. Boston, 1961. (See also No. 20.)

83. "A Conspectus of Dramatic Genres," *Kenyon Review,* Autumn, 1951, pp. 543–62.

84. "The Analogy of Democracy," *Bias* (Student Christian Movement of Canada), February, 1952, pp. 2–6.

85. "Poetry" (Letters in Canada 1951), *University of Toronto Quarterly,* April, 1952, pp. 252–57.

86. "Three Meanings of Symbolism," *Yale French Studies,* No. 9, n.d. [1952], pp. 11–19.

87. "Comic Myth in Shakespeare," *Transactions of the Royal Society of Canada* (Section II), June, 1952, pp. 47–58. Reprinted in *Discussions of Shakespeare's Romantic Comedy,* ed. Herbert Weil, Jr. Boston, 1966.

88. "Poetry" (Letters in Canada 1952), *University of Toronto Quarterly*, April, 1953, pp. 269–80. Reprinted in part in *Masks of Poetry*, ed. A. J. M. Smith, pp. 97–103. Toronto, 1962.

89. "Towards a Theory of Cultural History," *University of Toronto Quarterly*, July, 1953, pp. 325–41.

90. "Characterization in Shakespearean Comedy," *Shakespeare Quarterly*, July, 1953, pp. 271–77.

91. "Poetry" (Letters in Canada 1953), *University of Toronto Quarterly*, April, 1954, pp. 253–63.

92. "Poetry" (Letters in Canada 1954), *University of Toronto Quarterly*, April, 1955, pp. 247–56.

93. "English Canadian Literature, 1929–1954," *Books Abroad*, Summer, 1955, pp. 270–74.

94. "Poetry" (Letters in Canada 1955), *University of Toronto Quarterly*, April, 1956, pp. 290–304.

95. "La poesia anglo-canadiense," *SUR* (Buenos Aires), May–June, 1956, pp. 30–39. (Spanish translation by Jaime Rest.)

96. "The Typology of *Paradise Regained,*" *Modern Philology*, May, 1956, pp. 227–38. Reprinted in *Milton: Modern Essays in Criticism*, ed. Arthur E. Baker, pp. 429–46. New York, 1965.

97. "Towards Defining an Age of Sensibility," *ELH*, June, 1956, pp. 144–52. Reprinted in *Eighteenth Century English Literature: Modern Essays in Criticism*, ed. James L. Clifford, pp. 311–18. New York, 1959.

98. "Quest and Cycle in *Finnegans Wake*," *James Joyce Review,* February, 1957, pp. 39–47. (Title on cover: "Blake and Joyce.")

99. "Poetry" (Letters in Canada 1956), *University of Toronto Quarterly,* April, 1957, pp. 296–311.

100. "The Realistic Oriole: A Study of Wallace Stevens," *Hudson Review,* Autumn, 1957, pp. 353–70. Reprinted in *Wallace Stevens: A Collection of Critical Essays,* ed. Marie Borroff, pp. 161–76. Englewood Cliffs, N.J., 1963.

101. "Blake after Two Centuries," *University of Toronto Quarterly,* October, 1957, pp. 10–21. Reprinted in *English Romantic Poets: Modern Essays in Criticism,* ed. M. H. Abrams, pp. 55–67. New York, 1960.

102. "Blake's Introduction to Experience," *Huntington Library Quarterly,* November, 1957, pp. 57–67. (See No. 20.)

103. "The Language of Poetry," *Explorations,* No. 4, n.d., pp. 82–90. Reprinted in *Explorations in Communication,* ed. Edmund Carpenter and Marshall McLuhan, pp. 43–53. Boston, 1960.

104. "Poetry" (Letters in Canada 1957), *University of Toronto Quarterly,* July, 1958, pp. 434–50.

105. "Nature and Homer," *Texas Quarterly,* Summer-Autumn, 1958, pp. 192–204.

106. "Poetry" (Letters in Canada 1958, ed. by author), *University of Toronto Quarterly,* July, 1959, pp. 345–65.

107. "Poetry" (Letters in Canada 1959), *University of Toronto*

*Quarterly,* July, 1960, pp. 440–60. Conclusion reprinted in *Masks of Poetry,* ed. A. J. M. Smith, pp. 106–9. Toronto, 1962.

108. "The Structure of Imagery in *The Faerie Queene,*" *University of Toronto Quarterly,* January, 1961, pp. 109–27.

109. "Myth, Fiction, and Displacement," *Daedalus,* Summer, 1961, pp. 587–605.

110. "Varieties of Literary Utopias," *Daedalus,* Spring, 1965, pp. 323–47.

### E. REVIEW ARTICLES

111. "Canada and Its Poetry" (*The Book of Canadian Poetry,* ed. A. J. M. Smith), *Canadian Forum,* December, 1943, pp. 207–10.

112. "Turning New Leaves" (George Orwell, *Animal Farm*), *Canadian Forum,* December, 1946, p. 211.

113. "Blake on Trial Again" (Mark Schorer, *William Blake: The Politics of Vision,* and *The Portable Blake,* ed. Alfred Kazin), *Poetry: A Magazine of Verse,* January, 1947, pp. 223–28. Also, [Review] (*The Portable Blake,* ed. Alfred Kazin), *University of Toronto Quarterly,* October, 1947, p. 107.

114. "Turning New Leaves" (F. S. C. Northrop, *The Meeting of East and West*), *Canadian Forum,* March, 1947, p. 281.

115. "Toynbee and Spengler" (A. J. Toynbee, *A Study of History*), *Canadian Forum,* August, 1947, pp. 111–13.

116. "Turning New Leaves" (Ernst Jünger, *On the Marble Cliffs,* tr. Stuart Hood), *Canadian Forum,* March, 1948, p. 283.

117. "Turning New Leaves" (Reinhold Niebuhr, *Faith and History,* and Karl Löwith, *Meaning in History*), *Canadian Forum,* September, 1949, p. 138.

118. "Turning New Leaves" (*Don Quixote,* tr. Samuel Putman), *Canadian Forum,* December, 1949, pp. 209–11.

119. "Novels on Several Occasions" (novels by Ernest Hemingway, Budd Schulberg, William Goyen, Alberto Moravia, Charles Williams, Marcel Aymé, and Gheorghiu), *Hudson Review,* Winter, 1951, pp. 611–19.

120. "The Young Boswell" (*Boswell's London Journal, 1762–1763,* ed. F. A. Pottle), *Hudson Review,* Spring, 1951, pp. 143–46.

121. "Turning New Leaves" (*The Oxford Dictionary of Nursery Rhymes,* ed. Iona and Peter Opie), *Canadian Forum,* February, 1952, pp. 258–60. Reprinted in *Explorations* I, ed. Edmund Carpenter and Marshall McLuhan.

122. "Phalanx of Particulars" (Hugh Kenner, *The Poetry of Ezra Pound*), *Hudson Review,* Winter, 1952, pp. 627–31.

123. "Ministry of Angels" (review of books of criticism by Allen Tate, Herbert Read, and Francis Fergusson), *Hudson Review,* Autumn, 1953, pp. 442–49.

124. "Long Sequacious Notes" (Kathleen Coburn, *Inquiring Spirit*), *Hudson Review,* Winter, 1953, pp. 603–8.

125. "Art in a New Modulation" (Susanne K. Langer, *Feeling and Form*), *Hudson Review,* Summer, 1953, pp. 313–17.

126. "Turning New Leaves" (*Folk Songs of Canada,* ed. Edith

Fowke and Richard Johnston), *Canadian Forum,* July, 1954, pp. 89–91.

127. "Forming Fours" (C. G. Jung, *Two Essays on Analytical Psychology* and *Psychology and Alchemy*), *Hudson Review,* Winter, 1954, pp. 611–19.

128. "Myth as Information" (Ernst Cassirer, *Philosophy of Symbolic Forms,* Vol. I), *Hudson Review,* Summer, 1954, pp. 228–35.

129. "Content with the Form" (R. S. Crane, *The Language of Criticism and the Structure of Poetry*), *University of Toronto Quarterly,* October, 1954, pp. 92–97.

130. "An Indispensable Book" (René Wellek, *A History of Modern Criticism,* Vols. I and II), *Virginia Quarterly Review,* Spring, 1956, pp. 310–15. (Title supplied by editor.)

131. "Graves, Gods and Scholars" (Robert Graves, *Collected Poems*), *Hudson Review,* Summer, 1956, pp. 298–302.

132. "Poetry of the Tout Ensemble" (René Char, *Hypnos Waking*), *Hudson Review,* Spring, 1957, pp. 122–25.

133. [Review] *The Ulysses Theme,* by W. B. Stamford, and *Tragic Themes in Western Literature,* ed. Cleanth Brooks, *Comparative Literature,* Spring, 1957, pp. 180–82.

134. "Neo-Classical Agony" (Geoffrey Wagner, *Wyndham Lewis*), *Hudson Review,* Winter, 1957–58, pp. 592–98.

135. "Interior Monologue of M. Teste" (Paul Valéry, *The Art of Poetry*), *Hudson Review,* Spring, 1959, pp. 124–29.

136. "World Enough Without Time" (review of books by Jung,

Mircea Eliade, etc.), *Hudson Review,* Autumn, 1959, pp. 423–31.

137. "Nature Methodized" (Bonamy Dobrée, *English Literature in the Early Eighteenth Century*), *The Griffin,* August, 1960, pp. 2–11.

138. "The Nightmare Life in Death" (Samuel Beckett, *Molloy, Malone Dies,* and *The Unnamable*), *Hudson Review,* Autumn, 1960, pp. 442–49.

F. PUBLIC SPEECHES

139. "The Study of English in Canada," *Dalhousie Review,* Spring, 1958, pp. 1–7.

140. "Culture and the National Will," Convocation Address at Carleton University, May 17, 1957. Published by Carleton University for the Institute of Canadian Studies, n.p.

141. "Humanities in a New World," *University of Toronto Installation Lectures,* 1958, n.p. [pp. 9–24]. Reprinted in *Form and Idea,* ed. Morton W. Bloomfield and Edwin W. Robbins, pp. 162–81. New York, 1961.

142. "By Liberal Things," Installation Address as Principal of Victoria College, October 21, 1959. Toronto, 1959. 23 pp. Also in a soft-cover edition, untitled. Reprinted in *Acta Victoriana* and the *Varsity Graduate.*

143. "Literature as Possession," *Kenyon Alumni Bulletin,* January–March, 1960, pp. 5–9.

144. "Preserving Human Values," Address to the Social Planning

Council of Metropolitan Toronto, April, 1961. (Tape recorded and mimeographed.)

145. "Academy Without Walls," *Canadian Art,* September–October, 1961, pp. 296–98.

146. "The Imaginative and the Imaginary," *American Journal of Psychiatry,* October, 1962, pp. 289–98. ("Fellowship Lecture.")

147. "The Changing Pace in Canadian Education," The Norris Memorial Lecture at Sir George Williams University. Montreal, 1963, n.p.

148. "Elementary Teaching and Elemental Scholarship," Address given at the General Meeting in English (MLA) in Chicago, December 29, 1963. *PMLA,* May, 1964, pp. 11–18.

149. "Criticism, Visible and Invisible," *College English,* October, 1964, pp. 3–12.

G. OTHER WRITINGS

"Prelude" [a parable], *Canadian Forum,* September, 1941, pp. 185–86.
[4 untitled reviews] *Canadian Forum,* December, 1947, pp. 214–15.

Reply to a questionnaire on "The Classics and the Man of Letters," *Arion,* Winter, 1964, pp. 49–52.

Articles on "Verse and Prose" and "Allegory" in *Encyclopedia of Poetry and Poetics,* ed. Alex Preminger, Frank J. Warnke, and O. P. Hardison. Princeton, 1965.

### H. MANUSCRIPTS COMPLETED AND IN
### COURSE OF PUBLICATION

"Design as a Structural Principle in the Arts." Essay contributed to a *Festschrift*.

"Speculation and Concern." Essay contributed to a book on the humanities and the sciences, to be published by the University of Kentucky Press.

### I. MANUSCRIPTS IN ACTIVE PREPARATION

"Fools of Time: Studies in Shakespearean Tragedy." The Alexander Lectures for 1966, to be published by the University of Toronto Press.

A small book on Romanticism, commissioned by Random House, to be made up partly from three lectures on *Death's Jest-Book, Prometheus Unbound,* and *Endymion*.

An essay on Literature and Myth, commissioned by the Modern Language Association.

A book of documents in myth criticism, to be edited for the University of Chicago Press.

### J. EDITORSHIPS

General editorship of *The College Classics in English,* The Macmillan Company of Canada. Four volumes have appeared.

General editorship of a two-volume chrestomathy of English literature, to be published by Harcourt, Brace and World.


## An Index to the Subjects of Frye's Writings

Not all items have been read and a number have not been recently read. For these reasons some errors are probable. The major books often deal with many of these subjects but are listed only once.


1. Criticism

    A. Theoretical (including Myth, Archetype, Genre, Metrics)
        2, 3, 6, 13, 21, 30, 34, 35, 41, 43, 44, 49, 52, 63, 64, 68, 77, 78, 79, 80, 83, 86, 103, 105, 109, 110, 123, 125, 127, 128, 129, 130, 133, 136, 143, 146, 149

    B. Practical
        1. Blake
            1, 11, 17, 20, 23, 26, 27, 51, 82, 101, 102, 113
        2. Shakespeare
            7, 15, 37, 38, 39, 48, 87, 90
        3. Milton
            8, 9, 32, 96
        4. Other Major Writers
            5, 33, 36, 50, 72, 98, 100, 108, 112, 118, 120, 122, 124, 131, 135, 138
        5. Other Minor Writers (Non-Canadian)
            54, 74, 116, 119, 132, 134

6. The Other Arts
53, 55, 56, 57, 58, 59, 60, 62, 65, 66, 67, 73
C. Historical
19, 25, 42, 45, 89, 97, 114, 115, 117, 137
D. Canada and Canadian Culture
1. Arts and Letters
10, 12, 14, 16, 28, 29, 46, 70, 76, 81, 85, 88, 91, 92, 93, 94, 95, 99, 104, 106, 107, 111, 126
2. Canadian Society and Education
18, 47, 61, 139, 140, 145, 147

11. Social and Religious Thought

A. Education
4, 40, 69, 71, 121, 141, 142, 148
B. Religion and Society
22, 24, 31, 75, 84, 144

## II. A Checklist of Criticism of Frye's Work

### A. BIOGRAPHICAL NOTICES

Pelham Edgar, *Across My Path,* pp. 83–89. Toronto, 1952. (See Checklist, No. 10.)

A. S. P. Woodhouse, "Vignette LXIII," *PMLA,* May, 1961, p. i.

"About the Author," in Frye, *The Educated Imagination,* p. 159. (See Checklist, No. 4.)

B. REVIEWS AND DISCUSSIONS OF BOOKS

(For books the number of pages on which references occur is given, rather than transcriptions of indices.)

IA. Reviews of *Fearful Symmetry* (No. 1)

1947

[Review] *The New Yorker,* April 26, p. 97.

[Review] *Newsweek,* May 5, p. 102.

William Arthur Deacon, "Masterly Interpretation of William Blake's Poems," *Toronto Globe and Mail,* May 17.

"Sanity of Genius Is Found in Blake by Toronto Don," *Toronto Daily Star,* May 17.

John Garrett, "Turning New Leaves," *Canadian Forum,* July, p. 90.

Lloyd Frankenberg, "Forms for Freedom," *Saturday Review of Literature,* July 19, p. 19.

S. C———, "In Consideration of William Blake," *Christian Science Monitor,* September 27.

Kenneth Hamilton, [Review] *Dalhousie Review,* October, pp. 381–83.

Edith Sitwell, "William Blake," *The Spectator,* October 10, p. 466.

Ben Belitt, "Auguries of Energy," *Virginia Quarterly Review,* Autumn, pp. 628–30.

Herbert Marshall McLuhan, "Inside Blake and Hollywood," *Sewanee Review,* Autumn, pp. 710–13.

W. G., "William Blake," *Queen's Quarterly,* Autumn, pp. 395–97

Alfred C. Ames, "Escaping Selfhood," *Poetry: A Magazine of Verse,* November, pp. 101–3.

Geoffrey Keynes, "The Poetic Vision," *Times and Tide,* December 27, p. 1394.

## 1948

"Elucidation of Blake," *The Times Literary Supplement,* January 10, p. 25.

Helen W. Randall, "Blake as Teacher and Critic," *University of Toronto Quarterly,* January, pp. 204–7.

Fred Marnau, "William Blake," *New English Review,* February, pp. 100–101.

Blodwen Davies, "I Give You the End of a Golden String," *The Beacon,* February, pp. 314–19.

David V. Erdman, [Review] *ELH: A Journal of English Literary History,* March, pp. 9–10.

Josephine Nicholls Hughs, [Review] *The Thomist: A Speculative Quarterly Review of Theology and Philosophy,* April, pp. 257–59.

R. T. F. [Ralph Tyler Flewellig], "Blake Redivivus," *The Personalist: A Quarterly Review of Philosophy, Religion and Literature,* Spring, pp. 215–17.

Henry Wasser, [Review] *Modern Language Quarterly,* June, pp. 248–49.

Ivo Thomas, [Review] *Blackfriars,* August, pp. 395–96.

H. M. Margoliouth, [Review] *The Review of English Studies,* October, pp. 334–35.

1949

Edith J. Morley, [Review] *The Year's Work in English Studies,* XXVIII (1947), 219–20. London.

René Wellek, [Review] *Modern Language Notes,* January, pp. 62–63.

1960

Gene Lees, "Afterthoughts," *Downbeat,* December 22.

IB. References to Frye in Books of Blake Criticism

David V. Erdman, *Blake: Prophet Against Empire.* Princeton, 1954. 20 pp.

Stanley Gardner, *Infinity on the Anvil.* Oxford, 1954. 2 pp.

Hazard Adams, *Blake and Yeats: The Contrary Vision.* Ithaca, N.Y., 1955. 9 pp.

Vivian de Sola Pinto, ed., *The Divine Vision: Studies in the Poetry and Art of William Blake.* London, 1957. Includes one essay by Frye and references in two essays by others.

Robert F. Gleckner, *The Piper and the Bard: A Study of William Blake.* Detroit, 1959. 6 pp.

John E. Grant, ed., *Discussions of William Blake.* Boston, 1961. 2 pp. Includes two essays by Frye and references in five essays by others.

Harold Bloom, *Blake's Apocalypse: A Study in Poetic Argument.* Garden City, N.Y., 1963. 25 pp.

Hazard Adams, *William Blake: A Reading of the Shorter Poems.* Seattle, 1963. 31 pp.

Jean H. Hagstrum, *William Blake: Painter and Poet*. Chicago, 1964. 4 pp.

G. E. Bentley, Jr., and Martin K. Nurmi, *A Blake Bibliography: Annotated Lists of Works, Studies, and Blakeana*. Minneapolis, 1964. 6 pp.

S. Foster Damon, *A Blake Dictionary: Ideas and Symbols in William Blake*. Providence, 1965. One of twelve authorities cited.

Alicia Ostriker, *Vision and Verse in William Blake*. Madison and Milwaukee, 1965. 10 pp.

IIA. Reviews of *Anatomy of Criticism* (No. 2) and Discussions of Frye's Work as a Literary Theorist

### 1957

Leo Raditsa, [Review] *The Griffin*, August, pp. 18–23.

Vivian Mercier, "A Synoptic View of Criticism," *Commonweal*, September 20, pp. 618, 620.

Harold Bloom, "A New Poetics," *Yale Review*, Autumn, pp. 130–33.

M. B. [Maurice Beebe], [Notice] *Modern Fiction Studies*, Winter, p. 366.

### 1958

Paull F. Baum, [Review] *South Atlantic Quarterly*, Winter, pp. 140–41.

Kenneth Burke, "The Encyclopaedic, Two Kinds of," *Poetry: A Magazine of Verse*, February, pp. 320–28, esp. pp. 320, 324–28.

[Front Page], "Literary Dissection," *The Times Literary Supplement,* February 14, pp. 81–82.

Hazard Adams, [Review] *Journal of Aesthetics and Art Criticism,* June, pp. 533–34.

Frederick P. W. McDowell, "After the New Criticism," *Western Review,* Summer, pp. 190–96.

G. L. Anderson, [Review] *Seventeenth-Century News,* Summer, pp. 17–18.

George Whalley, "Fry[e]'s Anatomy of Criticism," *Tamarack Review,* Summer, pp. 92–98, 100–101.

[Review] *The Key Reporter,* July.

Margaret Stobie, "Mr. Fry[e] Stands Well Back," *Winnipeg Free Press,* July 26.

David Daiches, [Review] *Modern Philology,* August, pp. 69–72.

Walter Sutton, [Review] *Symposium,* Spring–Fall, pp. 211–15.

Eli Mandel, "Frye's Anatomy of Criticism," *Canadian Forum,* September, pp. 128–29.

Melvin J. Friedman, [Review] *Books Abroad,* Autumn, pp. 451–52.

Robert Martin Adams, "Dreadful Symmetry," *Hudson Review,* Winter, pp. 614–19.

1959

Erwin R. Clapp, [Review] *Western Humanities Review,* Winter, pp. 109–12.

M. H. Abrams, "Anatomy of Criticism," *University of Toronto Quarterly,* January, pp. 190–96.

George Whalley, [Review] *Modern Language Review,* January, pp. 107–9.

Thomas Vance, "The Juggler," *Nation,* January 17, pp. 57–58.

Hazard Adams, "Criticism: Whence and Whither?" *American Scholar,* Spring, pp. 226–38, esp. pp. 232, 238.

R. H. Reis, [Review] *Brunonia,* Summer, pp. 27–29.

E. W. Mandel, "Towards a Theory of Cultural Revolution: The Criticism of Northrop Frye," *Canadian Literature,* Summer, pp. 58–67.

Richard Kuhns, "Professor Frye's Criticism," *Journal of Philosophy,* September 10, pp. 745–55.

### 1960

T. S. Dorsch, [Review] *The Year's Work in English Studies,* XXXVIII (1957), 12. London.

### 1963

[Review] *Osmania Journal of English Studies,* III, 83–85.

Richard Poirier, "The Great Tradition" [review of the reissue of Scrutiny], *New York Review of Books,* December 12, p. 21.

### 1964

Letters of comment by John E. Grant and rebuttal by Richard Poirier, *New York Review of Books,* January 23, pp. 18–19.

Philip P. Hallie, "The Master Builder," *Partisan Review,* Fall, pp. 650–58.

Jackson B. Barry, "Fact or Formula: Comic Structure in Northrop Frye and Susanne Langer," *Educational Theatre Journal,* December, pp. 333–40.

Harold Bloom, *The Visionary Company: A Reading of English Romantic Poetry*. Garden City, N.Y., 1961. 24 pp.

Wayne C. Booth, *The Rhetoric of Fiction*. Chicago, 1961. 2 pp.

Frank Kermode, "Northrop Frye," *Puzzles and Epiphanies,* pp. 64–73. London, 1962.

Hazard Adams, *The Contexts of Poetry*. Boston, 1963. 7 pp.

René Wellek, *Concepts of Criticism,* edited and with an Introduction by Stephen G. Nichols, Jr. New Haven, 1963. 11 pp.

F. E. Sparshott, *Structure of Aesthetics*. Toronto, 1963.

Mary Curtis Tucker, "Toward a Theory of Shakespearean Comedy: The Contribution of Northrop Frye." Doctoral Dissertation, Emory University, 1963.

Walter Sutton, *Modern American Criticism*. Englewood Cliffs, N.J., 1963. 17 pp.

Angus Fletcher, *Allegory: The Theory of a Symbolic Mode*. Ithaca, 1964, 35 pp.

John Holloway, "The Critical Zodiac of Northrop Frye," *The Colors of Clarity: Essays on Contemporary Literature and Education,* pp. 153–60. London, 1964.

Murray Krieger, *A Window to Criticism: Shakespeare's Sonnets and Modern Poetics*. Princeton, 1964. 10 pp.

W. K. Wimsatt, *Hateful Contraries: Studies in Literature and Criticism*. Lexington, Ky., 1965. 14 pp.

Lee T. Lemon, *The Partial Critics*. New York, 1965. 7 pp.

III. Reviews of *The Well-Tempered Critic* (No. 3)

1963

Herbert Weisinger, "Victories in a Lost War," *The New Leader,* May 13, 3 pp.

## 1965

Douglas J. Stewart, "Aristophanes and the Pleasures of A
  *Antioch Review,* Spring, pp. 189–208, esp. pp. 191, 193

Wilhelm Grenzmann, "Der Zustand der Literaturkritik
  *der Zeit,* April 18.

Fred Inglis, "Professor Northrop Frye and the Academi
  of Literature," *Centennial Review,* Summer, pp. 319–3

J. F. Kermode [opinions as to the most important book pu
  in various fields during the preceding decade], *Ar*
  *Scholar,* Summer, p. 484.

Robert Weimann, "Northrop Frye und das Ende des New
  cism," *Sinn und Form: Beiträge zur Literatur,* XVII, N
  621–30.

Wayne Booth, "The Use of Criticism in the Teaching of l
  ture," *College English,* October, pp. 1–13, esp. pp. 4–8.

"Sons of New Critic," *The Times Literary Supplement,* N
  ber 25, pp. 1078–79.


IIB. Books Containing Discussion of *Anatomy of Criticism*
   Frye's Work as a Literary Theorist

R. S. Crane, *The Languages of Criticism and the Structur*
  *Poetry.* Toronto, 1953. 11 pp.

Donald Davie, *Articulate Energy: An Inquiry into the Synta*
  *English Poetry.* London, 1955. 13 pp.

William K. Wimsatt, Jr., and Cleanth Brooks, *Literary Criticis*
  *A Short History.* New York, 1957. 5 pp.

Harold Bloom, *Shelley's Mythmaking.* New Haven, 1959. 9 p

Munroe Beattie, "Critic Sees New Things in Familiar Writings," *Ottawa Citizen,* June 22.

[In "Reader's Guide"] *Yale Review, Summer,* pp. xx, xxii.

Earl Rovit, "The Need for Engagement," *Shenandoah,* Summer, pp. 62–65.

Eli Mandel, "The Language of Humanity," *Tamarack Review,* Autumn, pp. 82–89.

George P. Elliot, "Variations on a Theme by Frye," *Hudson Review,* Autumn, pp. 467–70.

[In "Notes on Current Books"] *Virginia Quarterly Review,* Autumn, p. cxxvi.

Anthony Ostroff, [Review] *Quarterly Journal of Speech,* December, pp. 457–58.

1964

A. J. M. Smith, "The Critic's Task: Frye's Latest Work," *Canadian Literature,* Spring, pp. 6–14.

Alvin C. Kibel, "Academic Circles," *Kenyon Review,* Spring, pp. 416–22.

William Blissett, [Review] *University of Toronto Quarterly,* July, pp. 407–8.

IV. Reviews of *The Educated Imagination* (No. 4)

1963

Eli Mandel, "The Language of Humanity," *Tamarack Review,* Autumn, pp. 82–89.

1964

Bruce Mickelburgh, [Review] *The Educational Courier* (Toronto), May–June, pp. 57–59.

William Blissett, [Review] *University of Toronto Quarterly,*
    July, pp. 406–7.
Simon Aronson, "Package of Ideas," *Chicago Maroon Literary
    Review,* October 23, pp. 6–7.


## 1965

Sherridan Baker, [Review] *College English,* January, pp. 329–30.
William S. Griffith, [Review] *Adult Leadership,* February, p. 262.
James Pierce, [Review] *English Journal,* April, p. 343.
Manfred Mackenzie, [Review] *Southern Review* (Australia),
    Vol. I, No. 3.
A. L., [Review] *Quartet,* June 5.
Alvin C. Kibel, "The Imagination Goes to College," *Partisan
    Review,* Summer, pp. 461–66.


## V. Reviews of *T. S. Eliot* (No. 5)

## 1963

Monroe Beattie, "A Wickedly Witty Essay on Eliot in New
    Series," *The Ottawa Citizen,* May 18.
J. B. Caird, "Writers and Critics," *The Scotsman,* June 22.
"Old Masters," *The Spectator,* July 5.
[Review] *The Times Literary Supplement,* July 12, p. 511.
Christopher Ricks, "Yes I Said," *The New Statesman,* September
    16.
Eli Mandel, "The Language of Humanity," *Tamarack Review,*
    Autumn, pp. 82–89.
A. H. Robertson, "T. S. Eliot," *Echoes,* October.

## 1964

William Blissett, [Review] *University of Toronto Quarterly,* July, pp. 403–5.

F. W. Watt, "The Critic's Critic," *Canadian Literature,* Winter, pp. 51–54.

VI. Reviews of *Fables of Identity* (No. 6)

## 1964

G. S. Fraser, "Mythmanship," *New York Review of Books,* February 6, pp. 18–19.

Denis Donoghue, "The Well-Tempered Klavier," *Hudson Review,* Spring, pp. 138–42.

Walter E. Swayze, "A Rich Experience," *Winnipeg Free Press,* May 30, p. 4.

Martin Price, "Open and Shut: New Critical Essays," *Yale Review,* Summer, pp. 592–94 (on Frye).

William Blissett, [Review] *University of Toronto Quarterly,* July, pp. 401–2.

Robert Alter, "Programmed Profundity," *Book Week,* July 19, p. 8.

Hayden Carruth, [Review] *Poetry,* September, p. 369.

James Reaney, "Frye's Magnet," *Tamarack Review,* Autumn, pp. 72–78.

## 1965

Robin Skelton, "The House That Frye Built," *Canadian Literature,* Spring, pp. 63–66.

VII. Reviews of *A Natural Perspective* (No. 7)

### 1965

Frank Kermode, "Deep Frye," *New York Review of Books,*
   April 22, pp. 10–12.

Christine Longford, "Bottom's Dream," *Irish Times,* June 12.

Martin Dodsworth, "Hit or Myth," *The Guardian,* June 18.

"As They Like It," *The Times Literary Supplement,* August 12.

Hayden Carruth, "People in a Myth," *Hudson Review,* Winter,
   pp. 607–12.

J. A. Bryant, [Review] *English Language Notes,* December, pp.
   134–36.

### 1966

Reuben A. Brower, "Myth Making," *Partisan Review,* Winter,
   pp. 132–36.

VIII. Reviews of Books Edited

a. *Sound and Poetry* (No. 13)

   Garff B. Wilson, [Review] *Quarterly Journal of Speech,*
      April, 1958.

   Hazard Adams, [Review] *Journal of Aesthetics and Art
      Criticism,* December, 1958, pp. 279–80.

   Irving Massey, [Review] *Canadian Music Journal,* Summer,
      1959, pp. 79, 81.

   Denis Donoghue, "Institutional," *Essays in Criticism,* July,
      1962, pp. 302–7, esp. pp. 302–4.

b. E. J. Pratt, *Collected Poems* (No. 14)

   F. W. Watt, "Edwin John Pratt," *University of Toronto Quarterly,* October, 1959, pp. 77–84.

c. Shakespeare, *The Tempest* (No. 15)

   I. B. Cauthen, [Review] *Shakespeare Quarterly,* 1960, pp. 79–80.

d. Peter F. Fisher, *The Valley of Vision* (No. 17)

   Ross Woodman, "Look!" *Alphabet,* December, 1962, pp. 80–82.

   D. R. Hauser, "Turning New Leaves," *Canadian Forum,* June, 1963, pp. 66–67.

e. *Design for Learning* (No. 18)

   John Pettigrew, "Illuminating Design," *Canadian Forum,* October, 1962, pp. 164–65.

   J. S. Erskine, [Review] *Dalhousie Review,* Summer, 1963, pp. 260–62.

f. *Romanticism Reconsidered* (No. 19)

   Marius Bewley, "Romanticism Reconsidered," *Hudson Review,* Spring, 1964, pp. 124–31.

   William Blissett, [Review] *University of Toronto Quarterly,* July, 1964, pp. 402–3.

   [Front page], "Poets of Their Time," *The Times Literary Supplement,* August 27, 1964, pp. 758–59.

   J. Baker, [Letter of comment on "Poets of Their Time" and reply from the reviewer] *The Times Literary Supplement,* September 10, 1964.

   R. H. Super, "Recent Studies in Nineteenth-Century Literature," *Studies in English Literature,* Autumn, 1964, p. 665.

   Mark Roberts, "Surprised by Lovejoy," *Essays in Criticism,* January, 1965, pp. 118–30.

Z. S. Fink, [Review] *Western Humanities Review,* Summer, 1965, pp. 273-75.

"Books of the 1960's—U.S.A." *The Times Literary Supplement,* November 25, 1965, p. 1084. (One of twenty-seven important books of literary criticism.)

IX. Reviews of Carl Klinck and others, eds., *A Literary History of Canada* (No. 46)

Eli Mandel, [Review] *Humanities Association Bulletin,* Spring, 1965, pp. 93-94.

George Woodcock, "The Long Day's Task," *Canadian Literature,* Spring, 1965, pp. 14-22.

Douglas Grant, "Canada's Literature," *Journal of Commonwealth Literature,* September, 1965, pp. 167-69.

A. J. M. Smith, "A Survey of English-Canadian Letters," *University of Toronto Quarterly,* October, 1965, pp. 107-16, esp. pp. 109, 114-16.

UTILIZATIONS, ADAPTATIONS, AND
MODIFICATIONS OF FRYE'S IDEAS

1955

James Reaney, " 'Toward the Last Spike': The Treatment of a Western Subject," *Northern Review,* Summer, pp. 18-25.

1957

James Reaney, "The Canadian Poet's Predicament," *University of Toronto Quarterly,* April, pp. 284-95.

## 1959

Jack M. Davis and John E. Grant, "A Critical Dialogue on Shakespeare's Sonnet 71," *Texas Studies in Literature and Language,* Summer, pp. 214–32.

Hope Arnott Lee, "New Horizons," *The English Exchange* (Toronto), Winter, pp. 5–7.

## 1960

James Reaney, [Editorial Statement of Policy] *Alphabet,* No. 1, September, pp. 3–4.

## 1961

Ihab Hassan, *Radical Innocence.* Princeton.

Dorothy Van Ghent, "Introduction," to Joseph Conrad, *Nostromo: A Tale of the Seaboard,* pp. vii–xxv; see p. xxvii. New York.

Graham Hough, "The Allegorical Circle," *The Critical Quarterly,* Autumn, pp. 199–208. See also his *Preface to the Faerie Queen,* New York, 1963, pp. 104 ff.

## 1962

Hazard Adams, "The Criteria of Criticism in Literature," *Journal of Aesthetics and Art Criticism,* Fall, pp. 31–34.

## 1964

Richard Ohmann, "In Lieu of a New Rhetoric," *College English,* October, pp. 17–22.

Paul Smith and Robert D. Foulke, "Criticism and the Curriculum," *College English,* October, Part I, pp. 23–30; Part II, 30–37.

Robert Scholes, "Two Theories of Narrative Literature." A paper of eleven pages, read before the General Topics 1, Poetics and Literary Theory, Conference Group at the 1964 Meeting of the Modern Language Association.

### 1965

James Reaney, "Search for an Undiscovered Alphabet," *Canadian Art,* September–October, pp. 38–41.

*Supervising Committee*

# The Program

SEPTEMBER 7 THROUGH SEPTEMBER 10,

1965

## Conferences

I. NORTHROP FRYE AND CONTEMPORARY
CRITICISM
Directed by Murray Krieger, University of Iowa

1. *Northrop Frye: The Critic in History*
Angus Fletcher, Columbia University

2. *The Language of Diagram: A Modest Inquiry*
W. K. Wimsatt, Yale University

3. *Ghostlier Demarcations*
Geoffrey H. Hartman, University of Iowa

II. THE EARLY 1590S AND THE EARLY
SHAKESPEARE
Directed by J. V. Cunningham, Brandeis University

1. *The Changes of Heroick Song: The Early 1590s and
Early Shakespeare*
Herbert Howarth, University of Pennsylvania
(prize essay)

2. *Lyric Style in the 1590s*
J. V. Cunningham, Brandeis University

3. *Shakespearean Mimesis, English Drama, and the Unity
of Time*
Norman Rabkin, University of California (Berkeley)

III. AMERICAN ROMANTICISM
Directed by Charles T. Davis, Pennsylvania State University

1. *The Inward Journey: A Romantic Theme for Bryant,
Poe, and Thoreau*
Charles T. Davis, Pennsylvania State University

2. *The Central Man: Emerson, Whitman, Wallace Stevens*
Harold Bloom, Yale University

3. *In the Country of the Blind: Hart Crane and American
Romanticism*
R. W. B. Lewis, Yale University

IV. SEXUALITY AND THE LIMITS OF LITERATURE
Directed by Steven Marcus, Columbia University

1. *Libertine Writing in the Augustan Age*
   David Foxon, The British Museum Library

2. *Sexuality and the Limits of Literature*
   William Phillips, Rutgers University

3. *Pornotopia: A Theoretical Discussion*
   Steven Marcus, Columbia University

4. *Sterne's Nasty Trifle: Sexuality as a Source of Literary Form*
   Robert Alter, Columbia University
   (prize essay)

# Registrants
## 1965

Kenneth T. ABRAMS, State University of New York (Stony Brook);
Ruth M. ADAMS, Douglass College; George R. ALLEN, Oxford University Press; Marcia ALLENTUCK, City College of New York; Robert ALTER, Columbia University; Hugh AMORY, Columbia University; Reta M. ANDERSON, Emory University; L. M. ANTALIS, The College of Steubenville; Mother MARY ANTHONY, Rosemont College; Richard W. ARTHUR, Rutgers University; George Wilbon BAHLKE, Middlebury College; Ashur BAIZER, Ithaca College; Sheridan BAKER, University of Michigan; Frank BALDANZA, Bowling Green State University; C. L. BARBER, University of Indiana; the Reverend J. Robert BARTH, S.J., Harvard University; L. A. BEAURLINE, University of Virginia; the Reverend John E. BECKER, S.J., Yale University; Florence BENNEE, Saskatoon Teachers College; James BENZIGER, Southern Illinois University; Sister Mary BERCHMANS, Maria College; John BERRYMAN, University of Minnesota; Jonathan BISHOP, Cornell University; Harold BLOOM, Yale Univer-

sity; Anne C. BOLGAN, University of Western Ontario; Muriel BOW-
DEN, Hofstra University; Brother C. Francis BOWERS, F.S.C., Man-
hattan College; the Reverend John D. BOYD, S.J., Fordham University; Frank BRADY, Pennsylvania State University; Michael BRIAN,
Sir George Williams University; Paul BRODTKORB, Jr., Hunter Col-
lege; R. A. E. BROOKS, Vassar College; Stephen J. BROWN, The
George Washington University; Ursula BRUMM, Free University,
Berlin; Audrey BRUNÉ, Sir George Williams University; Margaret
M. BRYANT, Brooklyn College; Mrs. W. BRYHER, Vaud, Switzer-
land; Jean R. BUCHERT, University of North Carolina (Greens-
boro); Brother Fidelian BURKE, F.S.C., LaSalle College; Sister M.
Vincentia BURNS, O.P., Albertus Magnus College; Douglas BUSH,
Harvard University; Mervin BUTOVSKY, Sir George Williams
University; Kathleen BYRNE, Seton Hill College; Grace J. CALDER,
Hunter College; John CAMERON, Amherst College; James Van
Dyke CARD, Franklin and Marshall College; Eric W. CARLSON,
University of Connecticut; Gale H. CARRITHERS, Jr., State Uni-
versity of New York (Buffalo); Sister MARY CHARLES, I.H.M.,
Immaculata College; Maurice M. CHARNEY, Rutgers University;
Hugh C. G. CHASE, Milton, Massachusetts; Irene H. CHAYES,
University of Maryland; Kent CHRISTENSEN, Upsala College; Sister
MARY CHRYSOSTOM, College of Mount Saint Vincent; Mother
Madeleine CLARY, O.S.U., College of New Rochelle; Mother MARY
CLEMENT, S.H.C.J., St. Leonard's Academy; James L. CLIFFORD,
Columbia University; Richard J. CODY, Amherst College; David
A. COLE, City College of New York; Susan A. COLE, City College
of New York; Sister Anne Gertrude COLEMAN, College of St.
Elizabeth; W. B. COLEY, Wesleyan University; Arthur N. COLLINS,
State University of New York (Albany); Rowland L. COLLINS,

Indiana University; Ralph W. CONDEE, Pennsylvania State University; John CONLEY, Queens College; Mrs. Robert COOK, Hobart College; G. Armour CRAIG, Amherst College; Martha CRAIG, Wellesley College; Lucille CRIGHTON, Gulf Park College; Charles R. CROW, University of Pittsburgh; John Murray CUDDIHY, New York City; J. V. CUNNINGHAM, Brandeis University; the Reverend John V. CURRY, S.J., St. Andrew-on-Hudson; Lloyd J. DAVIDSON, Virginia Military Institute; Charles T. DAVIS, Pennsylvania State University; Winifred M. DAVIS, Rutgers University; Robert A. DAY, Queens College; Charlotte D'EVELYN, Mount Holyoke College; George E. DORRIS, Queens College; Victor A. DOYNO, Princeton University; Mother M. St. Pierre DRUDY, College of New Rochelle; David A. DUSHKIN, Random House–Knopf, Inc.; Delbert L. EARISMAN, Upsala College; Edward R. EASTON, Pace College; Calvin R. EDWARDS, Hunter College; Thomas R. EDWARDS, Jr., Rutgers University; Frances ELDREDGE, Chatham College; Mother MARY ELEANOR, S.H.C.J., Rosemont College; Sister ELIZABETH MARIAN, College of Mount Saint Vincent; Scott ELLEDGE, Cornell University; Martha Winburn ENGLAND, Queens College; David D. ERDMAN, The New York Public Library; Sister MARY EUGENE, College of Mount Saint Vincent; Sister MARIE EUGENIE, I.H.M., Immaculata College; Robert O. EVANS, University of Kentucky; Doris V. FALK, Douglass College; H. Alfred FARRELL, Lincoln University; the Reverend Joseph J. FEENEY, S.J., Woodstock College; Sylvia D. FELDMAN, Emory University; Arthur FENNER, Jr., University of Detroit; Sidney FESHBACH, State University of New York (Stony Brook); Edward FIESS, State University of New York (Stony Brook); William J. FISHER, Rutgers University; P. D. FLECK, University of Western Ontario; Angus

FLETCHER, Columbia University; Edward G. FLETCHER, University of Texas; I. FLETCHER, University of Maryland; F. Cudworth FLINT, Dartmouth College; Claude R. FLORY, Florida State University; Ephim G. FOGEL, Cornell University; French FOGLE, Claremont Graduate School; George H. FORD, University of Rochester; Aldo FORTUNA, Holy Cross College; Elizabeth S. FOSTER, Oberlin College; Robert D. FOULKE, Trinity College; David FOXON, Queen's University; Richard Lee FRANCIS, Brown University; Ralph FREEDMAN, University of Iowa; Albert B. FRIEDMAN, Claremont Graduate School; Norman FRIEDMAN, Queens College; William FROST, University of California (Santa Barbara); Paul FUSSELL, Jr., Rutgers University; John H. GAGNON, Indiana University; Harry R. GARVIN, Bucknell University; John W. GASSNER, Yale University; Alexander GELLEY, City College of New York; Sumner GERMAIN, Franklin and Marshall College; A. B. GIAMATTI, Princeton University; H. K. GIRLING, York University; Donald E. GLOVER, Mary Washington College; Marshall H. GOLDBERG, Pennsylvania State University; Frederick GOLDIN, Rutgers University; Richard M. GOLLIN, University of Rochester; Sister MARY GONZAGA, R.S.M., Maria College; George GOODIN, Holy Cross College; David J. GORDON, Hunter College; Matthew GRACE, City College of New York; the Reverend Thomas J. GRACE, S.J., Holy Cross College; John E. GRANT, University of Iowa; James GRAY, Bishop's University; Robert A. GREENBERG, New York University; Donald J. GREENE, University of Toronto; Richard L. GREENE, Wesleyan University; Richard P. GREENLEAF, American University for Marxist Studies; M. E. GRENANDER, State University of New York (Albany); Ernest G. GRIFFIN, University of Alberta; Edward B. GROFF, Lincoln University; S. L. GROSS, University of Notre Dame; Allen GUTTMANN, Amherst College; Lawrence S. HALL, Bowdoin College; Robert G. HALLWACHS, Wells College; Robert HALSBAND, Columbia University; Victor M. HAMM, Marquette University; Mrs. William HANLE, Princeton University Press; Reginald L. HANNAFORD, Bowdoin College; Virginia HANS, Charles Scribner's Sons; Alfred B. HARBAGE, Harvard University; Richard HARRIER, New York University; David C. HARROP, Princeton University Press; John A. HART, Carnegie Institute of Technology; Geoffrey HARTMAN, Cornell University; Joan E. HARTMAN, Connecticut College; Carol HAWKES, Finch College; Harriet Bloker HAWKINS, Swarthmore College; Ann L. HAYES, Carnegie Institute of Technology; Allen T. HAZEN, Columbia University; Dennis V. HIGGINS, Tufts University; James L. HILL, Michigan State University; the Reverend William Bernard HILL, S.J., Novitiate of Saint Isaac Jogues; Frederick W. HILLES, Yale University; E. D. HIRSCH, Jr., Yale University; Laurence B. HOLLAND, Princeton University; Norman N. HOLLAND, Massachusetts Institute of Technology; Frank S. HOOK, Lehigh University; Vivian C. HOPKINS, State University of New York (Albany); Richard HOSLEY, University of Arizona; Donald R. HOWARD, University of California (Riverside); Herbert HOWARTH, University of Pennsylvania; Julia HYSHAM, Skidmore College; Sears JAYNE, Queens College; Wilfred T. JEWKES, Pennsylvania State University; Maurice JOHNSON, University of Pennsylvania; Leah E. JORDAN, West Chester State College; Robert M. JORDAN, State University of New York (Stony Brook); Joanne Spencer KANTROWITZ, Vassar College; George KEARNS, Harcourt, Brace & Company; A. L. KELLOGG, Rutgers University; Robert KELLOGG, University of Virginia; James G. KENNEDY, Upsala

College; Richard S. KENNEDY, Temple University; Sandra KER-
MAN, City College of New York; Karl KIRALIS, St. Lawrence
University; Joan Larsen KLEIN, Bryn Mawr College; H. L.
KLEINFIELD, C. W. Post College; Edgar H. KNAPP, Pennsylvania
State University; Maurice KRAMER, Brooklyn College; Murray
KRIEGER, State University of Iowa; the Reverend Joaquin C.
KUHN, S.J., Yale University; Lincoln F. LADD, University of North
Carolina (Greensboro); Parker B. LADD, Charles Scribner's Sons;
the Reverend John P. LAHEY, S.J., Le Moyne College; S. S. LAMB,
Sir George William University; John LAUBER, University of Al-
berta; the Reverend Henry St. Claire LAVIN, S.J., Loyola College;
Lewis LEARY, Columbia University; Oswald LEWINTER, Marist
College; R. W. B. LEWIS, Yale University; Christiaan T. LIEVES-
TRO, Drexel Institute; Carolyn M. LIGHT, University of Utah; Brita
LINDBERG, Uppsala, Sweden; Frank H. LINK, Freiburg Univer-
sity; George deF. LORD, Yale University; Marion K. MABEY, Wells
College; Isabel G. MACCAFFREY, Bryn Mawr College; Mary A.
MCGUIRE, Chatham College; Maynard MACK, Yale University;
Barbara MCKENZIE, Drew University; Richard A. MACKSEY, The
Johns Hopkins University; Charles A. MCLAUGHLIN, University
of Connecticut; Hugh N. MACLEAN, State University of New
York (Albany); Kenneth MACLEAN, Victoria College; Lorna E.
MACLEAN, Sir George Williams University; Mother C. E. MAGUIRE,
Newton College of the Sacred Heart; C. F. MAIN, Rutgers Uni-
versity; Roy R. MALE, University of Oklahoma; Steven MARCUS,
Columbia University; Mary H. MARSHALL, Syracuse University;
Edward A. MARTIN, Middlebury College; Harold C. MARTIN,
Union College; Jay MARTIN, Yale University; Louis L. MARTZ,
Yale University; John Kelly MATHISON, University of Wyoming;
Richard K. MEEKER, State University of New York (Potsdam);

Donald C. MELL, Jr., Middlebury College; John MIDDENDORF, Columbia University; Charles William MIGNON, University of Illinois; J. Hillis MILLER, The Johns Hopkins University; Lewis H. MILLER, Jr., Indiana University; Sister Jeanne Pierre MITTNIGHT, The College of St. Rose; Mother Grace MONAHAN, O.S.U., College of New Rochelle; Wesley A. MORRIS, University of Iowa; Julian MOYNAHAN, Rutgers University; Lowry NELSON, Jr., Yale University; Helaine NEWSTEAD, Hunter College; Eleanor L. NICHOLES, Harvard University Library; the Reverend William T. NOON, S.J., LeMoyne College; Robert O'CLAIR, Manhattanville College; Paul E. O'CONNELL, Prentice-Hall, Inc.; Mother Eileen O'GORMAN, Manhattanville College; Richard M. OHMANN, Wesleyan University; the Reverend Joseph E. O'NEILL, S.J., Fordham University; Tucker ORBISON, Bucknell University; Mother Thomas Aquinas O'REILLY, O.S.U., College of New Rochelle; Robert ORNSTEIN, University of Illinois; James M. OSBORN, Yale University; Charles A. OWEN, Jr., University of Connecticut; Ward PAFFORD, Emory University; Stephen C. PAINE, Salem College; Robert B. PALMER, Columbia University Libraries; Robert W. PARKER, Middlebury College; Roy Harvey PEARCE, University of California (San Diego); Norman Holmes PEARSON, Yale University; Marjorie PERLOFF, Catholic University of America; William PHILLIPS, Partisan Review; Michael David PLATT, Yale University; Klaus POENICKE, Yale Graduate School; Richard POIRIER, Rutgers University; Robert O. PREYER, Brandeis University; Max PUTZEL, University of Connecticut; Richard E. QUAINTANCE, Jr., Douglass College; Esther C. QUINN, Hunter College; Norman RABKIN, University of California (Berkeley); Paul RAMSAY, University of the South; Isabel E. RATHBONE, Hunter College; Joan REARDON, Barat College of the Sacred Heart; Compton REES, University of

Connecticut; Donald H. REIMAN, The Carl H. Pforzheimer Library; Irving RIBNER, University of Delaware; Keith N. RICHWINE, Western Maryland College; Mary L. RION, Agnes Scott College; Sister M. RITA MARGARET, Caldwell College for Women; Sister ROBERT MARY, O.P., Albertus Magnus College; William R. ROBINSON, University of Virginia; John H. ROBISON, State University of Iowa; Leo ROCKAS, State University of New York (Geneseo); Francis X. ROELLINGER, Oberlin College; Sister ROSE BERNARD DONNA, C.S.J., The College of St. Rose; Claire ROSENFIELD, Rutgers University; Angus ROSS, University of Rochester; William ROSSKY, Temple University; Kenneth S. ROTHWELL, University of Kansas; H. B. ROUSE, University of Arkansas; Rebecca D. RUGGLES, Brooklyn College; Irene SAMUELS, Hunter College; Bernard N. SCHILLING, University of Rochester; Helene B. M. SCHNABEL, New York City; Robert SCHOLES, University of Iowa; Flora Rheta SCHREIBER, New School for Social Research; H. T. SCHULTZ, Dartmouth College; Susan Field SENNEFF, New York City; Frank SEWARD, Catholic University of America; Richard SEXTON, Fordham University; Per E. SEYERSTED, Harvard University; Chester L. SHAVER, Oberlin College; Norman SILVERSTEIN, Queens College; Ernest SIRLUCK, University of Toronto; William SLOANE, Dickinson College; Paul SMITH, Trinity College; Nelle SMITHER, Douglass College; Susan SNYDER, Swarthmore College; Sister M. SOPHIA, Nazareth College of Rochester; George SOULE, Carleton College; Ian SOWTON, University of Alberta; J. Gordon SPAULDING, University of British Columbia; Richard STACK, Rutgers University; Arnold John STAFFORD, San Fernando Valley State College; Emily B. STANLEY, University of Connecticut (Hartford); Sister M. STEPHANIE, O.P., New York University; Maureen T. SULLIVAN,

University of Pennsylvania; Joseph H. SUMMERS, Washington University (St. Louis); Barbara SWAIN, Vassar College; Donald R. SWANSON, Upsala College; Peter A. TAYLOR, University of Connecticut; Ruth Z. TEMPLE, Brooklyn College; E. W. TERWILLIGER, Ithaca College; Sister M. THECLA, Seton Hill College; Wright THOMAS, New York State University College (Cortland); Sister THOMAS MARION, S.S.J., Nazareth College of Rochester; Michael TIMKO, Queens College; A. R. TOWERS, Queens College; R. C. TOWNSEND, Amherst College; Alan TRACHTENBERG, Pennsylvania State University; Donald TRITSCHLER, Skidmore College; Mary Curtis TUCKER, Marietta, Georgia; Helen M. ULRICH, Queens College; Thomas F. VAN LAAN, Rutgers University; Eugene B. VEST, University of Illinois (Chicago); David M. VIETH, Southern Illinois University; Sister VIVIEN, Caldwell College for Women; Eugene M. WAITH, Yale University; Andrew J. WALKER, Georgia Institute of Technology; Mother John Bernard WALSH, O.S.U., College of New Rochelle; Francis W. WARLOW, Dickinson College; Leslie C. WARREN, Canicius College; Elizabeth WATERSTON, University of Western Ontario; Herbert WEIL, Jr., University of Connecticut; George E. WELLWORTHY, Pennsylvania State University; James J. WEY, University of Detroit; Guy WHALLEY, Queen's University; James H. WHEATLEY, Trinity College; George WICKES, Harvey Mudd College; Brother Joseph WEISENFARTH, F.S.C., Manhattan College; Elizabeth WILEY, Susquehanna University; Frederick WILLEY, Boston University; Dorothy M. WILLIS, Bellport, New York; W. K. WIMSATT, Jr., Yale University; Martin WINE, Pomona College; Ross G. WOODMAN, University of Western Ontario; Samuel K. WORKMAN, Newark College of Engineering; Rose ZIMBARDO, City College of New York.